momofuku **milk bar**

Copyright © 2011 by MomoMilk, LLC
Photographs by Gabriele Stabile copyright © 2011
by Gabriele Stabile
All rights reserved.
Published in the United States by Clarkson Potter/
Publishers, an imprint of the Crown Publishing
Group, a division of Random House, Inc., New York.
www.crownpublishing.com
www.clarksonpotter.com

CLARKSON POTTER is a trademark and POTTER
with colophon is a registered trademark of Random
House, Inc.
Library of Congress Cataloging-in-Publication Data
Tosi, Christina.
    Momofuku Milk Bar/Christina Tosi. — 1st ed.
        p.   cm.
    1. Desserts.   2. Momofuku Milk Bar.
    3. Cookbooks.   I. Title.

TX773.T6684   2011
    641.8'6—dc22   2011007720
ISBN 978-0-307-72049-8
eISBN 978-0-307-95330-8
Printed in China
Book design by Marysarah Quinn
10 9 8 7 6 5 4 3 2 1
FIRST EDITION

momofuku milk bar

christina tosi

with courtney mcbroom
photographs by gabriele stabile
and mark ibold

Clarkson Potter/Publishers
New York

To Peter, Hannah, Oscar, and Hazel for putting this book in motion, for baking and eating and BabyBjörning and double dutching and doggy sitting

contents

foreword

When Momofuku Noodle Bar opened in 2004, we had no intention of ever serving desserts. We thought measuring out ingredients and baking was for wusses. Sometimes for regular customers we'd send out Hershey's Kisses or ice cream sandwiches that I would buy at the bodega across the street. We fooled around with an ill-advised and short-lived cupcake program for a second. Hiring a pastry chef was the furthest thing from my mind back in the day. I'd rather have hired an extra sous-chef than spend money on someone who spins sugar and bakes cookies. That's what I thought.

Then I met Christina Tosi.

The Department of Health had showed up at the restaurant and dumped bleach all over hundreds of dollars of pork belly we had stored in vacuum-sealed bags. The DOH required anyone cooking with a vacuum sealing system to have a Hazard Analysis and Critical Control Point (HACCP) plan, a crazy complex record-keeping system more common at food factories than ramen bars. Wylie Dufresne felt my pain and sent over Christina from wd~50, where she'd just implemented such a plan for him. She quickly and single-handedly saved us from DOH hell.

She was running these kinds of plans for several top New York City restaurants at the time, which would have been a full-time job in itself for most people. But I realized Tosi was not like most people and that we had a lot in common; she burns the candle at both ends and takes a flamethrower to the middle.

So I hired Tosi to help us organize our "office"—a desk in a hallway. Instead, she started organizing the company.

At the same time, she was working as a cashier at Ssäm Bar during the burrito phase, training for marathons at night, and somehow finding time to bake at home. Every day she came in to work she brought in something homemade—and amazing. Nothing tasted like it was made in a tiny Brooklyn apartment kitchen with no special ingredients and very little time. I practically lived on that stuff while we were trying to help Ssäm Bar transition from a failing Mexican-Korean burrito joint into something that would be around for more than a year.

Her cookies and pies, like many things that made their way onto the menus—the bo ssäms, the fried chicken dinner—started out just for the staff. I would constantly say she

should sell them; I was a broken record. I don't know what or when or how, but I must've worn her out. It seems like one day Tosi was writing up an HACCP plan and then she was making me promise never to buy desserts again for the restaurants. She had finally taken my hints about tackling a more culinary role at Momofuku. Even though it was five years ago, it seems like five minutes ago.

She knew how things worked by then and wasn't disappointed to bake in the basement . . . from the sugar, flour, and butter we already had on hand . . . after doing her "etc." job by day and running around the city doing HACCP plans for other restaurants . . .

Tosi has many talents: she is a dog whisperer; she can consume more sugar than seemingly humanly possible without keeling over; she is the most stubborn person I know. But it's her insane work ethic and brilliant mind that make her so special in my book.

I've always found that when you get talented people, you coach them up to a certain point and then let them loose. Tosi reset the bar in terms of that theory. Milk Bar wouldn't be—let alone be what it is—without her. This is the story of how it came to be and where it is now as she guides it into unknown territories.

One final word of advice before you dive in: Don't let her nice demeanor and southern charm fool you; underneath she is a ruthless killer . . . just like her recipes in this book, where deceptively simple flavors and ingredients combine in ways that make grown men whimper. Resistance to her sugar manifesto is futile.

David Chang

introductions are

awkward, especially in kitchens. Everyone's sizing each other up and no one wants to take the time to learn your name until you've been to the battle of dinner service enough nights in a row to show that you aren't going anywhere. The best way to get through it is to just throw your hand out there and share.

My name is Christina Tosi. I am twenty-nine. We opened Momofuku Milk Bar six days after my twenty-seventh birthday. I never thought I'd be where I am today.

I was born in Ohio and raised in Virginia. Both of my grandmothers are avid bakers, nurturing souls, and ferocious card sharks. The matriarchs of my family bake for every occasion, large or small—birthday, bake sale, and, more often than not, just because.

We are a kinship of sweet teeth on both sides of the family, some more refined and some more restrained than others. My mother cannot give up ice cream for the life of her, because she just can't bear the thought of having to go to bed on an "empty" stomach. My father was known to substitute a chocolate ice cream cone for any meal of the day.

I'm worse than either of them, to be honest. I've had a crippling cookie dough problem ever since I can remember.

My older sister and I were always allowed to help out in the kitchen. Like most kids, we would lick the beater from a batch of cookies. But for me, it was never enough. I would shape one cookie and then eat a handful of dough, or just eat the dough shamelessly until my grandmother caught on and chided me in her strident country-Ohio accent. I was always in big trouble, because I was going to do some combination of (a) spoiling my appetite, (b) making myself sick, and/or (c) getting salmonella poisoning. (She only invoked salmonella when I had managed to eat nearly an entire batch of cookie dough, which happened more often than I think she noticed.)

The old gals cut me off, and besides, it was high time I learned how to properly fend for myself. That's when I really started baking. I followed their same baking patterns. Baking was something that could, should, and did happen every day in my kitchen, too. Nothing went to waste and every baked good had character. Leftovers got incorporated into the following day's creation and each day became a challenge to put a new spin on an old favorite.

In high school and college, I fell madly in love with math and foreign languages. Baking was a hobby, not a profession. I worked at a restaurant while attending college in Virginia, waiting tables until they let me work as a morning prep cook. I

baked at my apartment in my off-hours every day, and I got my coworkers and schoolmates hopped up on my home-made desserts. I was the girl who always brought cookies or a pie or a cake. Always. Especially if it was somebody's birthday.

For two consecutive summers, a dear friend managed to convince the powers that be at a conference center on Star Island, New Hampshire, to hire me to help run their bakery. Breads and sweets for seven hundred people, three meals a day. Early mornings, late nights. I didn't talk to normal people about normal things; I baked and baked and baked, and I called my mom (and sister) every once in a while. I couldn't get enough of it.

One day on the way back from Star Island to Lacy Springs, Virginia, where I lived after college with friends who became family, I decided I'd move myself to New York City and go to cooking school. I looked on the internet and found the French Culinary Institute. Sounded good. Their rigorous pastry arts program was six months long—perfect for an antsy, overachieving student like myself.

I was going to school to study pastry in New York City, I told my family and friends as I began to plan my move

north. They weren't exactly dumbfounded—everybody knew how much I liked to bake—but I had only been to the city once before, a day trip when I was a teenager. And I'd never really talked about trade school; I had a good ol' college degree. But once I get an idea in my head, I'm hard to dissuade. I'm hardheaded to a fault.

While attending classes at the FCI by day, I worked as a hostess at Aquagrill by night to pay the rent and get a feel for a city restaurant. (Actually, I answered phones at the beginning, because they thought I was a joke; then they let me hostess once they saw I wouldn't let people walk all over me; and then I graduated to whatever the lady version of maître d' is—I actually wore a suit to work!) Soon after, I secured an externship that turned into a job at Bouley, under pastry chef Alex Grunert. The pastry cook who trained me at Bouley told me it would be the hardest job I'd ever have. And it kind of was, though after every hard day, I was ready to push it even further the next.

I tried dabbling in everything with any minute of free time. The city was all mine. I interned at *Saveur* magazine, because I thought I might want to be a food writer. I styled food and catered and consulted. I worked as a food runner at per se. But with each side job, I missed being in the kitchen.

I found myself walking into wd~50 one day and offering to work for free. (As long as I could make the rent with a paying gig, I would work for free anywhere in my free time.) Eventually they offered me a job.

I respected the chef, Wylie Dufresne, enormously. His approach to food was thoughtful, reasonable, logical, scientific. Every flavor pairing and composed dish had a purpose, an influence, and a level of independent thought that was revolutionary to my view of food. I grew the most as a cook while working there. Wylie, sous-chef Mikey Sheerin, and Sam Mason, the pastry chef to whom I reported, challenged me daily. Everything I cooked for family meal and everything I did to prep our pastry kitchen for service, setup, and breakdown was inspected, double-checked. If they had questions, I had to have answers, and "No, chef," or "I don't know, chef," were not words I ever liked to say.

I left the city after wd~50. I just had to get out. I had been pushing since I'd arrived four years earlier. I went back to Virginia first, spent time with the wonderful old gals in my life—Mom, Ang, my aunt Fran, my grandmas. I baked and I slept. I went to Thailand. Then I was ready to go back.

One day, Wylie's good friend David Chang, chef/owner of Momofuku, called about some issues he was having with the New York City Department of Health. One of the skills I'd acquired on the side was how to write a Hazard Analysis and Critical Control Point (HACCP) plan—a food-service safety plan that typically fills up a two-inch-thick binder—so that Wylie could cook sous vide without the city breathing down his neck.

I was just putzing around at that point, toying with the idea that writing HACCP plans would be the next phase of my "career." I knew I wanted to be in charge of my own kitchen, but I didn't think anyone would really hire me to be the head gal. I'm not really sure I believed I had enough vision/creativity/experience to be in charge of a pastry department, either. I was still a little too young and impressionable—and euphoric.

Dave quickly made an offer for me to be the "etc." of the small but growing team at Momofuku. I love me a good challenge, getting in on the ground floor and growing alongside everything and everyone else, moving and shaking, fighting an uphill battle—I love to organize, develop, figure it all out as a part of a team of believers. Momofuku Noodle Bar was a success at that point; Ssäm Bar was a burrito bar, not the restaurant it is today.

There was never a mention of kitchen work. It was more office stuff, or tit shit, as Dave and I called it. (I even worked the cash register!) Looking back, I think he secretly had a plan all along—he just knew I needed some time to grow into it.

I went to work, gave it my all, and came home to my oven and jars of sugar. I baked every night, and the next day I brought baked goods to the "office"—a glorified closet where Dave and I and two other people worked full time.

Dave would shovel the sweets into his mouth and joke about how I should start making desserts for the restaurants. We would laugh at how it would even happen. Who would plate desserts if we made them? And, more important, with a restaurant menu that was such a crazy hodgepodge of culinary approaches, what would we even serve? The idea of dessert seemed so far-fetched.

One day I brought in a toasted-miso crack pie, and Dave started in again. He started laughing and told me to go make a dessert for service that night. I laughed too, said, "OK," and went back to whatever office work I was doing. But then Dave looked at me and said, "Seriously, go make a dessert for service tonight."

I looked at him, slowly realizing he wasn't joking, and started hedging, "Well . . . But . . . I don't even know what I'd make. . . ."

He stared back, now stern and slightly cold. "Make this, or make those cookies. I don't care what the fuck you make. Just make something. And make sure it's fucking delicious."

I gave a quick head nod and let myself out of the office. I had no idea what I was going to do, but knew what I needed to do. And that's how our strawberry shortcake—simple, fast, and seasonal, the best thing I could come up with on short notice—was born. I think people who ate at Ssäm that night, people who were used to there being nothing for dessert but frozen mochi right out of the box, were excited that there was a new option. We sold some shortcakes. So the next day I made them again.

That's how it started. There were a lot of horrible mistakes that never made it to the menu. Some days I made five things that sucked. Then one day something would taste really good. And climbing up the hill became less painful than the downward spiral of failure.

I knew I wanted to draw on my influences, from both professional kitchens and home cooking adventures, and find a balance between the two. Mostly it was a challenge. To figure out what my voice was—how, stylistically, my food would translate. Luckily enough, Momofuku was the perfect home for desserts with no name, slightly confusing to some, but always thoughtful and delicious.

As a small restaurant group, with tight spaces and limited resources, we quickly learned that boundaries and limitations breed creativity. This always rang true for me, the one-person pastry department with no real prep table to call home.

There was no ice cream machine and no service freezer, just the walk-in freezer downstairs, a healthy jog from the upstairs service kitchen. There was no real heat source for baking anything to order—à la minute—or warming things for service. I prepped Ssäm Bar's desserts, and the garde-manger cook (the person doing oysters and appetizers) would plate and serve them. Garde-manger had eight to ten other menu items coming off their station on a given night; dessert was *not* a priority. I had to come up with recipes that were bulletproof. And the desserts had to appear thoughtfully composed, even without any of the elements that you typically get with dessert served at a fancy Manhattan restaurant.

So I came up with ways to make desserts seem larger than the sum of their parts: shortcakes and pies somehow became elevated into something more. Everyone in the kitchen would get their spoons in something before it made it onto the menu. And I would make sure that the recipe was just right before we served it. Once Ssäm had two steady desserts, I moved on to Noodle Bar.

Noodle Bar had already grown up and moved up the block from its original tiny space—which would later become Ko—into a spacious (by Momofuku standards) new location. I pushed as hard as possible for a soft-serve machine. I had been hell-bent on having dessert at the original tiny Noodle Bar, but it was a turn-and-burn operation. Diners would sometimes be in and out in an hour. So the idea of instituting a dessert program that would keep them in our tiny place for any longer than usual was not a popular one. But soft-serve was the easiest way for me to make dessert in bulk form, serve it quickly and affordably at the larger Noodle Bar location, and maintain a thoughtful perspective on food with interesting flavors—steeping milk was something I learned to love doing at wd~50.

Once Noodle Bar was running smoothly in its new location, Ko opened. We quickly flipped the space into a tasting-menu-only, online-reservations-only establishment. We had a lot of bad ideas for tasting-menu desserts, and deep down, I think Dave, Serp (Peter Serpico, the chef de cuisine, who runs the restaurant), and I knew I was just going to have to hide out in the Ssäm Bar basement and, come hell or high water, figure something out. The only productive thing that came from the original group meetings was a collaborative love affair with the idea of a deep-fried apple pie and the fact that I was going to need a little help in the form of an FCI extern. Enter Marian Mar.

Dave and a few other Momo guys went to the FCI career fair one day, mostly in search of savory cooks for their kitchens, and Dave promised he'd find me someone. Most people didn't even know the Momofukus served dessert, let alone thought of dropping off a pastry résumé. Except Marian.

Mar showed up at Ssäm Bar one night at 8 p.m. for the first night of her "externship" and helped me prep until about 2 a.m. We wore winter hats and turtlenecks because the basement was freezing. Giggled and figured shit out. This continued once or twice a week for the next few months. Little did either of us know Marian would become the anchor, lifesaver, soulmate, sister, and sous-chef who made and saved our little pastry department.

Mar stood next to me watching me pull out my hair trying to make a deep-fried apple pie. She looked at me like I was a little insane when, days before Ko was set to open, I told her about this cereal milk idea I had instead. I mean, I had to start looking at other options if I couldn't get the fried apple pie I promised figured out.

We tasted my next few attempts at an apple pie with Serp, as well as the cereal milk panna cotta I was working on. The panna cotta had a pretty boring banana cream with it, and he wanted something slightly different. He said, "I may be crazy, but what about avocado?" Both me and Mar perked up. Being a California girl, Mar loves avocados, and we'd really wanted to use them in a dessert. In fact, we had an avocado puree all ready, waiting for inspiration to strike. And there it was.

This is the essence of how we come up with things. We make things that we are interested in. We make them taste good. Then we stand in front of our fridge, with the door open, just like you do at home when you're trying to figure out what to make for dinner or eat for a midnight snack. We pick and pull out things we've been working on and see where we can merge ideas and flavors. We try to be intelligent about it. But most of the time, it's a eureka moment that we didn't even know we were working toward.

I finally came up with a deep-fried apple pie—a kind of take on the Hostess or McDonald's apple pies we all grew up on—through some messed-up, backwards, forget-every-thing-you've-ever-learned-about-pie-dough stroke of stupidity and kept moving. We opened our two-man pastry department at Ko by packing up five large pails of staple ingredients and a toolbox of equipment and moving them from Ssäm to Ko in the back of a lovely little '93 Subaru station wagon, the "company car."

Once we had a little prep table to call our own and more regularish hours, we began menu developing, putting better systems into place in the restaurants for our dessert programs, and, of course, making family-meal dessert daily. I developed a firm belief while working in restaurants in this city that family meal, the one prepared daily for your peers, is one of the most important meals you'll cook. The respect and integrity you put into it speaks very highly of you as a cook—and of how much you care about your fellow cooks. Often pastry is exempt from being required to contribute to family meal. But once I started full time at wd~50, I made it a personal requirement.

I would joke with anyone I worked next to that making family meal was my zen moment. I went back to my self-proclaimed roots; I baked without measuring (sacrilege

to most accomplished bakers) and used whatever mise-en-place was over- or underbaked or left over. Family meal is meant to be delicious and nurturing. I made what I knew from years of baking for myself—something I affectionately called crack pie because you can't stop eating it, cookies galore, brownies, etc. If there was a birthday within our three growing restaurants, I would make a layer cake with the same notion, using fillings we had on hand for our desserts.

Little did we know that making family-meal desserts with our in-house mise-en-place for the other restaurants would be recipe testing for our next project.

One day, tumbling down the stairs from the sidewalk into Ko's basement, Dave said, "Hey, if we could get you a bakery space, would you do it? The Laundromat next to Ssäm is closing, and we need to scoop up that space before someone else does."

"OK," I said. I'd come to realize that having a bakery was what I wanted as an end goal. I just didn't think it would come so soon.

"No, but seriously—if we could get that space for you to have as a bakery or something, would you really do it?" he asked.

"I said yes. I'll do it," I shot back, puffing up my shoulders.

It's funny to think that's how most of our big conversations go. They're quick and to the point. Dave and I get each

other, I think, on a level that most people don't, or maybe it's just that no one has understood either of us before. It's usually just a few sentences of dialogue; we figure out the hard stuff later. We are both people of our words, fearless of a challenge, and self-confident to a fault. We will do anything to make something work. It's one-half rock-hard work ethic, one-quarter pride, and one-quarter spite, I think.

With a skeleton crew of me, Mar, and Emily, an amazing Culinary Institute of America extern we picked up along the way, we began menu developing for a bakery that had no rules and no bounds. We would finish our daily prep for the restaurants as quickly as possible and make ourselves sick from testing and tasting thousands of versions of cookie dough, cake batter, and soft-serve ice cream bases.

A separate skeleton crew of Joshua Corey, our handsome "handyman" if you asked him his title, Dave, Drew Salmon, Momofuku's COO, and I began designing, contracting, and building out the space. We bought pendant lamps at walmart.com and contemplated what furniture, if any, should exist. None of us had ever opened a bakery, and the bakery I ran on Star Island was nothing like this, except I sure did know how to use an old eighty-quart mixer and wasn't afraid of scooping cookie dough out of it.

Long days turned into long nights, into yelling at contractors and slamming down phones. Our lives became mudding ceilings, sourcing the right nondescript display case, and painting the walls and ceilings in "hint of mint" when we should have been sleeping.

Only a small handful of people knew that Momofuku even had a pastry department, but we were determined to build a bakery that belonged to us, and we were going to do it as best we could. And by small handful, I mean really small. Milk Bar started with very few employees, working seven days a week, seventeen hours a day or more. Helen Jo joined our team for no good reason that I could see except that Marian, Emily, and my zombie-like state somehow enchanted her. James Mark, formerly the low man on the totem pole at Ko, who had baked a different loaf of bread for practically every family meal, became our overnight bread baker.

It wasn't long before the doors officially opened and the place was packed. Lines out into the cold all times of day. Customers were often confused by the crazy ice cream flavors we served morning till midnight, by the series of flavors that were always expanding and contracting, and we didn't begrudge them the confusion. We were making it up as we went along, but—and I can't express this more sincerely—we were truly surprised at how much people were into it. At a certain point, Anderson Cooper was plugging our crack pie on television. Things had turned surreal. Dave swears he knew it was going to work all along.

A year and a half passed. We opened our second Milk Bar location in midtown. Business was booming, but we were on top of each other, mixing and baking from 7 a.m. to 2 a.m. in 700 square feet of space. We'd hoist sheet pans of cookie dough over the heads of our patrons several times a day to get them to a refrigerator to chill for an hour or two before we hoisted the pans back to our oven to bake off for the evening and late-night crowds.

We needed a bigger boat. There are only so many chest freezers from Craigslist you can squeeze into an already cramped basement, so many cookie fridges you can surreptitiously put out on the floor of Milk Bar, and so many tables you can take over for shipping and special orders while telling guests they have to stand somewhere else to eat their slice of pistachio layer pie.

We found and signed a lease on a huge warehouse space that would be our castle, our kingdom, our home. Cue noise: car screeching to a halt. Only thing is, it wouldn't be rezoned and kitchen-ready for another four months.

So we chose the next best (and only other) option: schlepping our kitchen up to Spanish Harlem to bake in a stranger's fourth-story rental kitchen, using a stranger's dingy refrigerators, a stranger's elevator that always seemed to break down when the deliveries

were obscenely large, and, even worse, a stranger's wonky ovens.

And there we perched, in a barely-air-conditioned 90- to 100-degree kitchen for a long summer. We baked, and we developed a delivery system, a packaging system, an "oh, shit" list to keep us on top of every single disaster we could and surely did encounter at 113th Street and Third Avenue. We were in boot camp all over again. We climbed those stairs with fifty-pound bags of flour on our shoulders or wobbled down them with twenty-four-quart tubs of soft-serve ice cream to take to Noodle Bar. We screamed, we sweated. We tried to hide it when we were down at the restaurants. We scrubbed sheet pans at 3 a.m. until we hired and trained a dishwashing staff. We carpooled up and down the FDR Drive at all hours of the morning and night.

Then, just when the summer of 2010 cooled off, our new kitchen in Williamsburg, Brooklyn, was ready. And by ready, I mean empty, clean, and ready for us to do it all over again, one more time.

We painted the creepy rooms with leftover paint from everyone's past home painting experiments (mostly mine), hung pictures of dogs and Teenage Mutant Ninja Turtles on the empty walls, and assembled enough prep tables and metro shelves to fill thousands of square feet. My mother, aunt, and sister stuffed my poor brother-in-law's truck full of yard-sale furniture to cart across state lines for our

makeshift offices. We made friends with big guys with big dollies and trucks with lifts. And we rented U-Haul trucks and moved our ever-expanding kitchen from Spanish Harlem to our home. Finally.

After just two years, we caught up on sleep (kind of). We wooed an amazingly talented staff to join us in our plight. Each one of us has a different background, a different attitude, and a different view on life and food.

Helen Jo stuck by my side, whether we were spray-painting a rusty dough sheeter gold and naming her Beyoncé, running outside to pet a puppy, or commanding an entire kitchen to work faster! Leslie Behrens entered full force with blonde like you have never seen before, and a love for key lime pie turned cake that let us know she was a lifer. Yewande Komolafe, our wanderlust Nigerian princess, reminded us daily to be fierce with attitude and never to miss an episode of *This American Life*. Helen Hollyman, with her patience and hilarity, taught us how to wrangle quirky customers with grace and poise while laughing inside all the way. Sarah Buck danced into our basement and schooled us in the art of bouncing to Reggaeton while corralling a sassy staff into banging out a prep list in record time. Courtney McBroom, cool as a cucumber, hilarious, and vulgar to a fault at times, is my mighty kitchen stand-in, silently reminding me it will all be OK, even if I take a day off (she's also half of the hilariousness of this text). Maggie Cantwell, equally nosy and hungry at all times, now runs

our operations and reminds us to be good women, girlfriends, and wives, all while balancing spreadsheets and telling cooks what it was like when she was in the kitchen. Louis Fabbrini, the tall, dark, and handsome Doogie Howser of Milk Bar, has somehow managed to know and love the cause among a jungle of crazy women and balance a delivery staff, an etc. staff, a technology infrastructure, and a Milk Bar world-domination scheme, all at the age of twenty-two and then twenty-three. Alison Roman, our West Coast transplant, is so ridiculous in spirit, chatter, and skill that we just give her some jars to fill with jokes or drama—or her next amazing batch of flavored butter, jelly, or jam. Alex Wilson, God bless her, flies strong and solo most of the time, ricocheting off each Milk Bar, and generally managing our laughter levels, homemade apron distribution, cookie pars, and locations all the while.

We are a family. We call each other out on bullshit, push each other to be better everythings, and catch each other when it all blows up in our faces. We have lost sanity and sleep over new desserts. We argue about and challenge the ways we make each recipe, the way we serve each item, the way we get each dessert to you with the shortest line and in the friendliest way possible.

The heart of our daily lives at Milk Bar is the core of this book—warm, hardworking, strong, humble, and straightforward. I'm excited and scared to share it with you. We are no geniuses. Putting it down on paper for someone else to read leaves us vulnerable to the ease that is the essence of our desserts' success.

There are no tricky secrets to what we do—it's about getting in there, working smart, and making something delicious out of everyday ingredients. The only things you need that are not already in your cupboards are a few funny ingredients that will make you shake your head in disbelief. Our recipes exist to appeal and to relate to everyone.

We all started off as home cooks, and we never stray far from our roots. This cookbook is a collection of the recipes from our lives and love affairs with food that we have adapted, adjusted, tasted once and tasted twice, and made in the Momofuku spirit. They are simple and tasty. They are salty and sweet. If you ever wanted to start a pastry department, then open a bakery, then grow an empire out of a few employees, young by birth or at heart—or just turn on your oven and make something super-tasty—you really only need the ten mother recipes you'll find here. Honestly, that's how we did it.

real talk

In our kitchen, **real talk** means we break it down for you. Good-bye niceties: just cold, hard truths is what real talk is all about. When one of us is not doing the right thing, copping a bad attitude, feeling sorry for him- or herself, being lazy, or underperforming (we're all human), we all know what's needed to get each other back on track. Real talk.

So. Here's how it's going to go. I'm surrendering all of my favorite recipes to you. Letting you into our world. We are a tight-knit, loving bunch, unafraid of eating too much cookie dough or of slathering our bread with too much butter. We are our own breed of home bakers with formal educations, and we strive to make thoughtful, clever food that hits home every time. We work hard. We laugh hard. We love to share our takes on baked goods with anyone and every-one. We are incredibly casual but never cavalier. We are deadly serious and deadly accurate when it matters. Spend some time understanding how we laid out this cookbook, read our ridiculous mantras, understand the need for certain ingredients and kitchenware—and you will be one of us.

Cooking any of the recipes in this book is like working a day at Milk Bar side by side with us. But before you're even given a time card to work in our kitchen, you have to pass the ultimate test. Are you a hardbody?

hardbody is a term we use at Milk Bar to describe a person who goes above and beyond. Softbodies need not apply in our kitchen. (We like softbodies as people, we just don't like working next to them.) Every single person who works with us is either a hardbody or a hardbody-in-training.

A hardbody never complains—a hardbody isn't afraid to work through the toughest of times. No heat in the winter? Snowsuits under your chef's whites. No AC in the summer? Sweat to the oldies and keep working. No elevator, no room for the one hundred gallons of organic milk to be delivered, a flat tire on the van, a broken dolly? No prob-lem. We are hardbodies. We got it.

Maybe you're mixing a huge batch of cookie dough and your industrial-size mixer shits the bed. A softbody would surely give up. But not a hardbody. You've never lived until you've mixed one hundred pounds of compost cookie dough by hand and then raced to scoop it with your lunatic boss. Just ask Heather Pelletier. The people need their cookies!

A hardbody approaches each recipe and task with a sense of humor. A hardbody keeps cool and keeps creative. As

you read through this book, you'll find that a striking number of these recipes were the result of burning, or mismeasuring, or just throwing some leftovers into the mixing bowl. A hardbody knows there's always a brilliant recipe waiting to be invented with leftover Ritz crunch or overproofed mother dough.

Everybody gets a hardbody litmus test before they become one of us. Once they've shown us their hardbody potential, they are allowed through our doors and let into the fold. They are officially a part of Milk Bar. They are family.

clocking in at Milk Bar means showing up. You put on your kitchen whites, pull your hair back, and get your notebook and Sharpie out to make a prep list and plan your day of baking. Turn on some tunes and get in the zone.

To get started at home, you need to clock in too—make sure you and your kitchen are ready to dedicate some time to the food. You've got to make the kitchen you're about to bake in your own. Put on your favorite album, or tune your radio in to NPR. Have your favorite oven mitts, apron, and head scarf ready. Hang pictures of puppies all over the place. It matters—I promise.

This cookbook is designed to help make your life in the kitchen easy. Get yourself organized before you start. Understand how the cookbook works. Understand how we work. Know what recipes you want to make.

You must know what you're about to get into before you get into it. In our kitchen, prep lists and clipboards abound (thirty-three is the current count—more clipboards than employees), to get each other up to speed once we've clocked in, so that we're not lost in a sea of sugar and sheet pans when we start our day.

In French cooking, there are four "mother sauces." Most every French sauce is a derivative of one of these four sauces. It is a known fact that if you master the mother sauces, you can make nearly anything in French cooking. I like to think the same is true of the Milk Bar pastry kitchen.

I flew solo at the beginning, but as the restaurants slowly grew, so did the techniques and dessert menus. I had to be smart about prep work and mise-en-place. We built three pastry departments, three retail bakery locations, and one sweet stronghold out of ten mother recipes—nine sweet ones and one bread dough.

Start with a mother recipe and discover the range of desserts that stems from that recipe. Following the mother recipe in each chapter are recipe variations, where the main ingredients and flavor profiles change but the technique remains more or less the same.

Next to some recipes, you will see sidebars, or references to the hows and whys of a given technique or an ingredient used in the recipe. Recipes used beyond a single chapter—in recipes you can find elsewhere in this book—are also noted, to give you ideas, to help you find new ways to use your favorites. We're setting you up real good.

"Setting yourself up for success" is a phrase we love to use seriously and sarcastically alike in the kitchen. When someone doesn't wash the mixing bowl or leaves you without enough cornflakes to make cereal milk, they are not setting you up for success, and you let them know it. Loudly. But mostly we use it sarcastically, because we love being aware of one another and really value setting ourselves and each other up for a successful day in the kitchen.

To set yourself up at home, first decide what you want to accomplish. Are you making cookies for a bake sale or planning a fancy dinner party for later in the week, or do you just want to try out a few mother recipes and keep them in your fridge or freezer for a snack (or until you're ready to master the art of the Cereal Milk Ice Cream Pie, page 59, or the Chocolate Malt Layer Cake, page 139)? Once you've determined that, make yourself a prep list. Organize your recipe(s) before you actually start. Baking can seem difficult when you try to do too much at once. Some recipes take a little longer to execute, but they're well worth the commitment. Plan for this when you clock in.

ingredients

We choose our ingredients for many different reasons—be it flavor, ease of use, or the result in a final recipe. Both Milk Bar and Momofuku in general have always been about in-your-face flavor. We rarely make anything that is soft, gentle, or quiet. It's almost always loud.

Here are the whys and why nots of every ingredient, along with a lot of baking tips and tricks of the trade. This isn't a throwaway section, a snooze fest. Educate yourself and read on. Can't find an ingredient at your local grocery store or specialty food mart? Never underestimate the power of the internet.

baking powder and baking soda

We do pretty classic American baking, so we stick to good ol' baking powder and baking soda to give our cookies and cakes a little bit of lift. We use them in our cookies to help control spread, to help them brown, and to keep them balanced in flavor and texture. We like an aerated cookie that's crispy on the outside and fudgy in the center. We use double-acting baking powder exclusively. Any brand of baking soda will do—just make sure you don't use the baking soda that you keep in the refrigerator to soak up all those stinky smells (unless, of course, you like your blueberry cookies to taste like leftover Indian food).

butter

We love butter at Milk Bar. I grew up with a mother who used only margarine, which is tragic, because butter makes or breaks the quality of a baked good. We spend a lot of money on really good butter, and we've never changed the kind we use. Plugrá is a European-style butter made from cultured dairy, which makes it that much tastier. Its butterfat content is 82 percent (the average stick of grocery store butter is 80 to 81 percent), and it's very yellow. So, if your cookies turn out pale, we'll all know you cheated. Always opt for unsalted butter, so you can control the amount of salt in your baked goods.

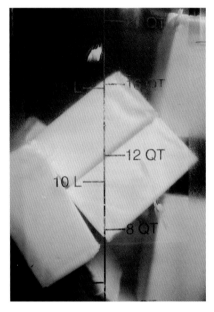

chocolate

Valrhona is a delicious, dependable chocolate, whether you are using it for chocolate work or in baking. The first real pastry chef I ever worked for used Valrhona. He swore by it, and I followed suit. We use fèves or pistoles (discs or chips) of this fancy chocolate because they're easier to measure, portion, and melt down than the large gold-bar-like slabs of gourmet chocolate you often see.

I like Valrhona's 72% Araguani chocolate the most. It's a really nice dark chocolate—not too bitter, with slight floral notes that allow you to do more delicate things with it if need be, but it also bakes off with taste and

integrity, letting everyone know it's a high-quality chocolate. The 55% Valrhona is a great semisweet chocolate; it's not too milky, and it's not too sweet. I feel the same way about the versatility of Valrhona's white chocolate; it's not too cloying, and it doesn't taste too much like cocoa butter or vanilla, as many white chocolates do.

chocolate chips, mini

We use Barry Callebaut semisweet mini chocolate chips. They are the perfect size and flavor. We always use these tiny chips because they give you a little chocolate chip in every bite of any cookie or cake they're used in.

citric acid

You can find citric acid marketed as sour salt in the spice aisle at many grocery stores. We use citric acid most often to enhance the flavor of our seasonal recipes. It's not hard to find, so please don't skip it. Though you can use lemon or lime juice for tartness in its place, citric acid doesn't impart any flavor and it doesn't add liquid to the recipe—its greatest allure.

cocoa powder

Don't mess around with cocoa powder. We use Valrhona brand. It is a Dutch-processed, or alkalized, unsweetened cocoa powder, meaning it has been treated with an alkali to neutralize its acidity. If you are going to use grocery store cocoa powder, don't expect your chocolate desserts to look or taste as dark and fudgy as ours.

eggs

Every egg that we call for in this cookbook is a large egg. We get them from a nearby Pennsylvania Dutch farm. Find fresh eggs from a local farm if possible; just remember that their shells are typically thinner than that of your average grocery store egg—so be careful, or strain your eggs through a fine-mesh sieve once cracked to be sure no shards of shell remain. Save extra yolks or whites—there are plenty of recipes that call for one or the other.

extracts and food coloring

One of the first things I learned at wd~50 is that Wylie hates food extracts (and food coloring). He believes people rely on them as crutches, which can be true, especially on the savory side. However, extracts are much more common in the pastry field. Because of working with Wylie, I always feel like I have to explain myself twenty times, so here goes: At Milk Bar, we don't use extracts (or food coloring) excessively, and we certainly don't use them as a crutch. When we use them, it's always for a really good reason, usually just to enhance a flavor that we've already put into something.

Peppermint extract (used in our mint cheesecake and mint glaze) provides 100 percent peppermint flavor; fresh mint doesn't give you the same cooling, deep mint flavor as the extract. Fresh mint also oxidizes, turning brown when you bake it. Of course, Wylie would probably say something like, "You should figure out a way to make it green with spinach juice." But spinach-juice cheesecake just doesn't sound as good. Hope I didn't let you down, chef.

Bananas are not yellow when they are cooked down and used in a cake or cream—or ice cream—they are brown. And nobody wants to eat a brown cake, cream, or ice cream. We don't use an ungodly amount of food coloring; and if you don't want to use it at all at home, you don't have to. But guess what? You are going to be face-to-face with a brown banana cream pie or banana cake, and that's a fact.

feuilletine

Feuilletine, French in origin, is tiny flakes of impossibly thin, seemingly toasted crepe bits. We use Cacao Barry feuilletine in the nut crunch recipes; it is a natural partner to nut-based pastes. Feuilletine is an ingredient worth seeking out (in specialty baking stores or at amazon .com) and having in your kitchen because of its insane, one-of-a-kind texture. There is really no substitution for it; cornflakes or Rice Krispies do not produce the same results.

One thing to note about feuilletine: it gets soggy if you put it in a liquid that isn't 100-percent fat-based—enter Dave Chang, who likes to stumble into the pastry kitchen, take a scoop

of feuilletine, pour milk over it, and inhale it in seconds, just before it turns to mush.

flour

Originally we developed all of the Milk Bar recipes using generic all-purpose flour. And, in fact, all of the recipes in this book were tested with regular all-purpose. That said, when we could afford to do so, we upgraded to better stuff. So now our "all-purpose" flour is actually King Arthur Bread Flour. The choice is yours. We tried a lot of different varieties of King Arthur flours in our recipes, but we really loved the results with their bread flour best.

Because our cookies have such a high butter ratio, we like the extra protein content of bread flour to help bind them together. I would never have guessed that the high protein content would make such a difference, but it does. It's one of those secrets. Only thing is, when making the cookies, you must be vigilant about not overmixing the dough. If you mix it even a little too long after adding the flour, the protein in the flour will start to develop gluten and your finished product will resemble a

tough bread ball, not a tender buttery cookie.

For *cake flour,* we've never been able to find one that we like better than Purasnow. We've tried a few different "pastry" flours, and those will work, but we really like the way that the General Mills cake flour comes out in our recipes. There is something about it that gives the cakes an undeniable flavor and an all-American sponginess. It's available in grocery stores. (Do not use self-rising cake flour.)

freeze-dried corn
Get regular freeze-dried corn from Whole Foods, amazon.com, or justtomatoes.com. They all offer an organic version, but it's not the same in flavor or color. We grind the corn down to a powder in the blender before we use it, so do the same in your kitchen. Make sure you store it in an airtight container, because otherwise moisture will get to it, and it will make you very sad.

fruit purees and juices
You can purchase fruit purees or you can buy whole seasonal fresh fruit and make a puree at home. I don't consider purchasing already pureed

fruit cheating, especially if you want to make White Peach Sorbet (page 131) in the dead of winter. Passion fruit puree in particular is definitely worth sourcing; trying to make it at home will test your endurance and nerves. It is also cheaper to buy it already processed.

There are several options when it comes to sourcing purees; my favorite, as always, is amazon.com. We use Boiron and Capfruit, both widely distributed. Figure out what brand of puree you like best and go for it.

If you choose to make fruit purees at home, it is essential that you use the ripest fruit possible; if you don't, there is no way the final result will taste good. There are a few things, though, that you will have to make from scratch. Concord grape juice, for the PB & J Pie (page 63), is one of them. Buying the sugary commercial stuff is not an option; you can't make that concession.

Never use fruit juice or fruit nectar in place of a puree. The solids and water contents are different and the recipe will not come out the same.

gelatin
I was taught to use sheet gelatin in culinary school because it's easier to store, measure, bloom (or soften), and melt, so that's what we use in our kitchen. Gelita Silver Strength gelatin sheets are the common currency in pastry and savory kitchens in NYC. However, powdered gelatin can be substituted for sheets in every case, and every recipe in this book that calls for gelatin includes the conversion. You will by no means sacrifice quality if you use powdered gelatin. Whatever you use, though, you must bloom the gelatin correctly, or your results will definitely suffer. Follow the instructions on page 29.

glucose
Glucose is an invert sugar that we use in many recipes. We use it in liquids to add body and reduce the chance of crystallization. We use it in ice creams to keep them soft and smooth, even after they've been in the freezer for a while. We use it to give our cookies their signature fudgy centers and crispy edges, and it also increases their shelf life. We use it in ganache to keep it smooth, adding viscosity and fullness and helping to bond the ingredients. So many glorious things happen through the wonder and beauty of glucose.

You can substitute half the amount of light corn syrup for the glucose in these recipes, but be forewarned that corn syrup is looser and way sweeter; it will get you close, but the end result won't have exactly the same flavor or consistency as what we make in our kitchen. Glucose syrup is easily found on amazon.com. Go ahead and order a bucket. You're worth it.

graham crumbs

Graham crumbs are a brilliant invention of the graham cracker manufacturers. They took all of their broken graham cracker bits that they couldn't sell whole and made their own market for them, which I think is genius. I often wonder whether they were also the geniuses behind the whole cheesecake-must-have-a-graham-crust phenomenon. We prefer Keebler graham crumbs.

heavy cream

When we call for heavy cream, there is no substitution. It is one of the key ingredients of crack pie. We use it in our Graham Crust (page 112). We use it in our ganache recipes (see page 205). Heavy cream has ridiculously cool emulsifying properties. You can use cold heavy cream to bind any dairy-based product that has broken or been overwhipped. If you are making Banana Cream (page 91), for example, and you walk away from your mixer while whipping the cream,

only to return to find stiff peaks where soft peaks should be, all you have to do is gently stir a small amount of cold heavy cream into the mix, and it will magically turn the hard peaks back into beautiful, soft, billowy peaks.

Get your heavy cream from a local farmer if possible. Milk Thistle (see page 46) can't keep up with the amount of heavy cream we go through in a week, but their product is a delicious one that we would always use if we could. Just be sure to shake that farm-fresh cream well before using.

marshmallows

We use Kraft mini marshmallows. We use mini marshmallows for the same reason we use mini chocolate chips: to get a little bit in every bite. If you only have large marshmallows, you can cut them up, but that's a really big pain in the butt.

milk

Milk Bar. Clearly, a lot of our stuff is dairy-based. I was raised on skim milk by a mother who was very concerned about my cholesterol level. That is probably why I rarely drank milk growing up. In fact, I only had it when it was dousing Lucky Charms. As an adult, I refuse to use skim milk in any of my recipes and I scoff at the idea of 2%. All of our recipes are designed around whole milk. If you cut out the fat, you are going to cut out the flavor.

We love supporting our favorite local organic farmer, Dante Hess at Milk Thistle farms in Ghent, New York (see page 46). If you can't find a local dairy, it's OK to use store-bought milk—just make sure it's whole.

milk powder

Do not use milk powder to make milk. I repeat: do not add water and stir; it's gross. Trust me, my dad used to try to make me drink milk made from milk powder when I was little.

Instead, think of milk powder as MSG for bakers. MSG doesn't taste like anything; it just makes everything taste better. Milk powder works in the same way. We use it in recipes because it has an amazing way of adding a terrific baseline flavor. We also use it to increase the milk solid content in ice creams, which results in a milkier, denser, and silkier ice cream. I also like what it does in certain baking recipes. For example, it adds chewiness when you put it in a cookie.

We do use milk powder for its stand-alone flavor in our milk crumbs (page 74). We use white chocolate in the recipe to give it a sweeter, milkier taste, but the milk powder is what really determines the flavor.

miscellaneous dairy

We call for a lot of different dairy products in this cookbook—things like yogurt, sour cream, and goat cheese. But we don't get too fancy in our kitchen with these, because we spend so much money on expensive butter and whole milk. You can certainly use an artisanal sour cream or yogurt to support your local economy. Whatever you buy, just make sure to get the full-fat option.

I really love sour cream. Sour cream with brown sugar was one of my favorite snacks as a kid. Its fat content is similar to that of heavy cream, so you can paddle it, and it will come to soft or heavy peaks. I like Friendship sour cream just fine.

nonstick cooking spray

There are lots of approaches to greasing pans. My grandmother and mother save butter papers and use the residual butter on them to grease pans. In our kitchen, we use Pam spray for everything, because it is easy and convenient.

nuts

My mom never puts nuts in anything, but somehow she magically has these creepy bags of nuts that sit in her pantry for God knows how long. They're usually stale and sometimes rancid. Make sure the nuts in your kitchen have not gone the same way! A rancid nut probably won't kill you, but it will make a huge difference in the quality of your food. You should always store nuts in the fridge if you don't think you are going to use them right away, and you should definitely taste them before you make anything with them.

We use Bazzini brand nuts. If you can get pieces instead of whole, they're usually cheaper, and if you're going to use them for a brittle (see page 167), you're going to break them down,

anyway. We get our nuts skinned and blanched, so there isn't any of that weird brown skin on them.

nut pastes and butters

Nut pastes and butters aren't cheap. And the more you spend on them, the better the quality you'll get. Pistachio and hazelnut pastes typically have a percentage of sugar added to them, which we love. Almond butter does not. Any specialty cooking or baking store should have a supply, or there's always the internet. We use Bazzini brand almond butter, Valrhona hazelnut paste, Skippy peanut butter, and Agrimontana pistachio paste.

oats

We keep it classic with Old-Fashioned Quaker Oats. They are easy to find in the grocery store; just don't accidentally buy instant or quick-cooking oats. We go through oats very quickly, but you probably won't go through the whole container at once. So make sure you store any that you have left over in an airtight container or a zip-top plastic bag to prevent little bugs, like weevils, from trying to crawl in and snack on them.

oil

We use grapeseed oil in all of our baking. It is a little more viscous than most vegetable oils, it doesn't impart any flavor, and it has an amazing emulsifying quality. I could watch it emulsify liquid in fat forever. If you have canola oil in-house, though, feel free to use that; just don't use oil that's so viscous it barely pours, or oil that is water-thin.

pectin

We use pectin, specifically pectin NH, a powdered pectin often used in fruit- and water-based pastry glazes; it's easily obtained online. Pectin NH gels quickly with liquids and does not impart any flavor, color, or fogginess in the process. It gives a much better

consistency than what you get setting something with gelatin, which makes something jiggly like Jell-O. When using pectin, we always mix it with a portion of the sugar and salt from the recipe so it doesn't clump up when we whisk in the liquid. Pectin must be brought to a boil and simmered for a minimum of 2 minutes to fully hydrate and activate it in the liquid it is gelling.

pretzels

We use Snyder's mini pretzels for every recipe that calls for mini pretzels. We use these small ones for the same reason we use mini marshmallows and mini chocolate chips: you get a wider distribution of their flavor and a little bit in every bite, plus it's super-cute to see a whole pretzel peeking out of a compost cookie.

salt

We use kosher salt, which has larger granules than iodized table salt. There is something about iodized salt that I don't like flavorwise. Plus it is really small and it can be confused with sugar, and that scares me. Kosher salt is usually located on the shelf right near the iodized salt at the grocery store. Please use it; it's so much better.

spices

Treat your spices with love and care. They aren't going to go bad, but don't use a spice that's been sitting around for five years in your pantry along with some rancid nuts and old rainbow jimmies. As far as the kind of spices we use, I'm a straightforward McCormick girl. If you have a grinder and the time, and you want to freshly grind whole spices, go for it, but if you already have them powdered, there's no shame in that.

sugar

We use classic Domino sugar. Also, it's local—the plant is literally right down the street from our kitchen. We don't use superfine sugar, just the regular old granulated stuff.

We also use Domino confectioners' sugar (also known as powdered sugar at home, or "10X" in the trade) and light and dark brown sugars. We don't use dark brown sugar very often because I'm not a huge fan of its outright deep, dark molasses flavor.

vanilla extract

We use two different kinds of vanilla extract, brown Patisse brand and clear McCormick brand. Neither is of any fancy caliber, but we use these specific vanilla extracts on purpose because they are the flavor that most people relate to in their baked goods. Vanilla beans and fancy vanilla paste do not taste like home to me, but commercial vanilla extract does.

We use brown (standard) vanilla extract in 90 percent of our baked goods. It's the extract that flavors nearly every homemade chocolate chip cookie. We use clear McCormick vanilla extract for the Birthday Cake (page 105), Birthday Cake Crumb (page 78), and Birthday Cake Frosting (page 107). It is vanilla in flavor, but not flavored by any actual vanilla beans. It's "vanilla" in more of a guilty tub-of-frosting, box-cake way. The two are not interchangeable in recipes. Both Patisse brown extract and McCormick clear vanilla are available online.

vinegar

The main vinegars you will find in this cookbook are sherry, rice wine, and distilled white. Each has its own nuances, and we use each for a reason—kind of like when people pair wine with food. We use vinegars to bump up flavor intensity or add balance to a recipe. I like sherry vinegar with cherries or deep red berries. Distilled white vinegar is perfect in our red velvet cake. And, of course, we use apple cider vinegar for anything involving apples or pears.

yeast

Our Mother Dough recipe (page 222) calls for active dry yeast. Be sure to keep it in an airtight container and store it in the refrigerator. Active dry yeast has an expiration date, and nothing is worse than spending a lot of time making a beautiful bread dough that will never rise because you used dead yeast.

The equipment

The ‎equipment in our kitchen is, in part, what sets some of our techniques and final products apart from others. In many instances, we've eliminated the process of tempering eggs (see page 26) or simplified the method of making an ice cream base (see page 29) with the use of a simple appliance such as a hand blender or countertop blender. We're not going to tell you you need keep that blade on your chef's knife sharp (sorry, Dave) or that you need a slab of marble to temper chocolate properly. We've simplified our equipment needs to the necessities and their substitute counterparts.

acetate

We use sheets of acetate to assemble all of our cakes, building the layers up in a cake ring. We leave the cakes bare on the sides because we spend a ton of time developing the colorful layers and textural nuances, so why in god's name would we want to hide them under a layer of frosting? The acetate gives you clear walls to build within and leaves a really pretty, shiny edge once it's removed. It's important to peel the acetate off while the cake is still frozen, because if it is at room temperature, or even refrigerated, the sides of the cake will stick to the acetate and it won't have that clean smooth edge. You can buy acetate sheets at craft stores, some stationery stores, some office-supply stores, and online.

bench scraper

If you buy a good-quality metal bench scraper, then you've just bought yourself a new best friend, especially where the crumb and mother dough chapters are concerned. A bench scraper is all you need to break up crumbs, portion the mother dough, and clean up the kitchen counter in a cinch when you are done.

blenders

We use a commercial Vita-Prep blender, a vital part of our kitchen, all day, every day. But there is no need to buy a blender as expensive as a Vita-Prep. All you need is a dependable blender, and if you already have one, that will do fine.

We use an inexpensive hand blender, sometimes known as an immersion blender, to mix all of our milks and ice cream bases. We also use it to blend ganache to keep it smooth without heating it up or incorporating air into it. If you don't own a hand blender, you are missing out on simplifying tasks and easy cleanup.

brushes

I always buy cheap pastry brushes. We've bought expensive brushes, and they go missing or deconstruct just as quickly as the cheaper ones. Keep one brush that you use only for pastry. You never want to use the same brush to egg-wash bread dough that you used to brush baby back ribs on the grill. Wash the brush in the dishwasher or soak it in hot soapy water for a few minutes. Once

it gets really raggedy (which it will), boil it in a pot of water for 10 minutes to bring it back to life. We replace brushes when we notice they are starting to shed their bristles.

cake rings

Every cake recipe in this book calls for baking the batter in a quarter sheet pan, then using a 6-inch cake ring (which you build the cake in) to cut out rounds. A cake ring is basically a cake pan with no bottom. If you already have a 6-inch cake pan, though, you can use that to cut the rounds and to build the cake. You can find cake rings at amazon.com, starting at $5.95.

chinois

The chinois, also known as a China cap, a fine-mesh strainer, or a sieve,

is a piece of equipment that we live and die by. There is no substitution for one; it is the last line of defense to ensure a supersmooth product with little mess. A chinois is a conical strainer that tapers toward the bottom, so you can strain cereal milk or lemon juice into the smallest of vessels with no spillage. Get the finest-mesh chinois you can.

containers

We use quart and pint plastic containers; the ones that are synonymous with take-out Chinese soup. They are clear, airtight, and extraordinarily valuable, because they will increase the shelf life and freshness of whatever they're holding. It's really important that the containers you use to store desserts aren't the same ones that you store raw onions or leftover spicy beef from Taco Tuesday. Nobody wants to eat cornflake crunch that tastes like Ortega's taco seasonings. And if you don't use an airtight container, after day one, your food is going to taste like your refrigerator—and chances are your refrigerator smells like old cheese and water-packed ham.

food processor

We use an industrial-strength food processor, called a Robot Coupe. It costs around $800 new, and it's rare to find them used because they last forever. By no means do you need to use a Robot Coupe in your home kitchen, but you definitely need a food processor of some sort for grinding down crumbs for pie crusts or grinding nut brittles into almost a powder. If you don't have one, you should get married so you can put one on your registry. (In fact, you should probably just convince someone to marry you so you can put all of the equipment listed in this section on your registry.)

gloves

We use gloves not only because the New York City Department of Health and Mental Hygiene requires us to do so, but also because we like to keep our hands clean. Molding a chocolate crust into a pie tin with bare hands is a bad idea: you'll be scrubbing chocolate out from under your fingernails for weeks. We like disposable latex gloves for the easiest cleanup.

ice cream machine

We don't have an ice cream machine. We use soft-serve machines at the Milk Bars and at Noodle Bar, and we use a Pacojet for everything else.

The Pacojet is a European marvel that takes a frozen block of sorbet or ice cream and shaves it down into tiny layers, all the while incorporating air into it, so that the final product comes out like it was just spun in an ice cream machine—except it only takes ninety seconds. The only problem with Pacojets is that they cost nearly five grand. No joke.

So, we did you the honor of re-creating all of our soft-serve and Pacojet recipes so that they work in a home ice cream maker. We used a Donvier ice cream machine (readily available at amazon.com) to test all of the recipes. If you have the ice cream attachment for the KitchenAid stand mixer, that is another good one to use.

ice cream scoop

If you want to make cookies that look like our cookies, you need to buy a no. 16, 2¾-ounce NSF blue-handled ice cream scoop. Scoop ice cream onto plated desserts with the same blue scoop, or use it to portion out brioche dough (see page 236). The scoops are simple to track down online and not too expensive.

knives

The knife of a pastry chef is notoriously dull. Make no mistake, our knives aren't any different, but we only sharpen them when it comes time to break down a chicken for family meal or to dice two cases of apples. I use a paring knife for almost everything, but you will also need a larger chef's knife for a few of the recipes in the book. I recommend a 5-, 6-, or 7-inch chef's knife; the most important part in choosing one is making sure you feel comfortable with its size.

ladle

We use a ladle to help pass things through a chinois, and that's pretty much it. We use a 2- or 3-ounce ladle; anything else is too big to fit inside the bottom of the chinois. But, while a ladle makes things easier, if you don't have one, you can use the back of a spoon instead.

microwave

We don't have a stovetop (we have one lowly induction burner), and I am mad for microwave ovens. We use our microwave for everything from melting butter and chocolate to heating liquids before adding bloomed gelatin to them. The microwave is one of man's greatest inventions, and it is the cleanest and easiest way to apply heat to a world of desserts. Make sure you use a microwave-safe bowl. It's important to note that, depending on the size and age of your microwave, it will heat more quickly, slowly, powerfully, or feebly than ours. Get to know your microwave. When melting anything in a microwave, don't power it up for 3 minutes and walk away. Check on anything you are microwaving at 15- or 30-second intervals, stirring each time to ensure a gently melted or warmed-through ingredient.

mixer and attachments

You need a stand mixer, and you need the paddle, hook, and whisk attachments. A handheld granny mixer won't work for this cookbook. A lot of our recipes require mixing dough for an extended amount of time; plus, most of the cookie doughs are way too heavy for a granny mixer. We use a Brevel, but you could use a KitchenAid, a Viking, or a Sunbeam.

molds and vessels

Our favorite molds are made of silicone. They make it easy to unmold and to clean. They certainly aren't necessary—our desserts taste the same regardless of what shape they're molded into—but they make plated desserts seem more composed and classy. The Saltine Panna Cotta (page 191), for example, calls for a 2-ounce round mold. We tried to change it up for you at home, though; you can set the Cereal Milk Panna Cotta (page 37) in 5-ounce juice glasses from your cupboard.

parchment paper

We get parchment paper in sheets that perfectly fit our full-sized sheet pans. You can get by with using wax paper, or use a Silpat if you have one. Just don't use aluminum foil; it conducts more heat and will burn the bottom of your cookies.

peeler

A peeler is not a necessity, but it will make your life a lot easier when it comes to peeling apples, carrots, potatoes, and things of that nature. As with a chef's knife, make sure you choose a peeler you are comfortable holding in your hand.

pie tins

We use 10-inch disposable aluminum foil pie tins that are 1 inch deep. We use disposable tins because of the insane number of pies we bake off every day. If you already have a 9-inch pie tin, you can totally use it; just keep in mind that when you are molding a crust or filling it you may need to adjust the measurements and bake times (where applicable) slightly. If you're giving away pies left and right, though, you should definitely use disposable ones so you don't have to remember which friend ended up with your cute pie plate.

plastic wrap

Professional plastic wrap is a necessity. Saran Wrap is a flimsy joke. We use Purity Wrap Food Service Film, which you can buy at amazon.com. It is inexpensive, wraps around anything, and keeps everything inside its force fields fresh. Once you use this stuff, you'll never go back to supermarket brands.

pots and pans

We love All-Clad—their pots are the best. They have heavy bottoms that rarely cause anything to burn. To cook from this book, you need three heavy-bottomed pots or saucepans: a small one that holds 1 to 2 quarts, a medium one that holds 3 to 4 quarts, and a large one that holds 4 to 6 quarts.

rolling pin

There is a wealth of pie recipes in this book, but not a single one of them involves rolling out pie dough with a rolling pin. I think that's pretty cool. You will only need a rolling pin for the Cinnamon Bun Pie (page 152) and the mother dough chapter (page 218) and to break up pieces of nut brittles (page 167) before you grind them down. That's it.

scale

One of the main messages of this cookbook is to be precise when it makes a difference and not to sweat things when it doesn't. When measuring ingredients for any recipe, precision makes a huge difference. If you spend the money on this cookbook and take the time to read it, do yourself a favor and invest in a $30 scale that measures grams, one of the most accurate measurements you can take in a kitchen. To be nice, we still give you "freedom measurements" (see page 26) for each weight, but I can't emphasize enough how much more perfect and uniform your desserts will turn out if you weigh the ingredients in grams. Treat your scale with love and respect. Never store anything on top of it, and make sure it stays calibrated. We check our scales once a week by placing a pound of butter on each of them to make sure they read 453 grams (that's 1 pound, or 16 ounces, or 2 cups butter to all of you non-gram speakers).

sheet pans

My mother has really horrible, thin, wobbly baking sheets. I was just as guilty in my home kitchen too, until I snuck two home from the bakery one day. Invest in good-quality, heavy, rimmed sheet pans: one 10 × 13-inch "quarter sheet" pan for cakes, and one or more 13 × 18-inch sheet pans called "half-sheet" pans in the trade for cookies and everything else. Treat them with the same integrity and respect that you do for the mixing process of cakes and cookies, because that sheet pan is what the success of the final product is based on. Wash and store them with the same esteem.

silpat

A Silpat is like a piece of parchment paper, except that it's made of silicone and you can use it over and over again. It's a nonstick mat for sheet pans. You can use it to bake cookies, or to pour caramel or brittle onto and let it harden. Make sure you have one that matches the size of the sheet pan you have. Hand-wash your Silpat in warm soapy water with a nonabrasive sponge or even a washcloth.

sound system

Our sound system consists of five mismatched $10 plug-into-the-wall speakers. We all listen to music while we work. It makes the hard times seem so good. It's how we set the tone in the kitchen and get comfortable. If I'm feeling tired and I know I have an uphill battle, I always listen to rhythmic, upbeat music. I'm also a

huge fan of Neil Young and Bob Dylan, because there is something about their music that is calming and nurturing; it reminds me of being at home. I love the mellow, whiny, dream-like stuff because it kind of speaks to my imagination. I find it an interesting study in human science to hear what other people like to listen to while baking.

spatula

A heatproof spatula is a great investment, and it is a necessity for the nut brittle chapter. You start each nut brittle recipe by making a dry caramel, using your heatproof spatula (I don't like using wooden spoons). It is very versatile, and you can use it for so many different things—hot or cold. All you need is one.

spoons, tasting

When you make something, always have four or five clean spoons nearby so that you can taste as you go and adjust the recipe accordingly, then taste again (see page 26). Plus, it's a great excuse to eat raw batter.

tape

Specifically, blue tape. Painters were really onto something when they came up with it. The stuff sticks, but then it comes off and doesn't leave a mess. Amazing. We use it to label everything that we make. We use a Sharpie marker to write the name of the item, the date it was made, and the initials of whoever made it on the tape.

thermometers

We use two different types of thermometers: one for our ovens and a digital one for when we make Peanut Butter Nougat (page 178) or Italian meringue (see page 198). An oven thermometer is essential for getting uniformly consistent baking results every time. The digital thermometer is key in getting the sugar to just the right temperature before pouring it into egg whites. Having both types of thermometers is nonnegotiable.

timer

Unless you keep an inner time that's on par with the atomic clock, you are going to need a timer for anything that gets baked (unless, of course, you have a dependable oven timer).

whisk

You need a whisk. It's a great way to homogenize a mixture. Get a typical French wire whisk, and you'll be set.

techniques

Listen, we're only really fussy about the techniques that will make or break your desserts, the difference between bready lumps-of-coal-like cookies and our buttery, lacy domes of heaven. So read on for the Milk Bar accelerated pastry program and the techniques that truly make a difference.

God bless . . . freedom measurements

I run a kitchen where a new recipe will be tested five times with 2-gram increments of a certain ingredient until we hit the perfect proportions. When writing this book, however, I knew I would have to give measurements that the average home cook or baker would recognize—meaning in cups and spoons. But everyone knows that one person's "packed" brown sugar is not another's. It hurt my heart a little to have to give what can be such incredibly variable measurements.

Europeans use the metric system, lovely precise measurements. What are our cups and spoons even called? Late one night, after staring at recipes and a computer screen for far too long, we decided to call them "freedom measurements." The recipes in this book were developed in grams and tested in both their metric and freedom incarnations. We have done our best to give the most accurate freedom-measurement equivalent to each gram quantity. If you want your recipe to be exact, buy a small scale and get to baking in grams; if you want to get remarkably close, free yourself with freedom measurements.

cookie sizes and shapes

There's only one size at Milk Bar: not too big, not too small. But I suppose I could understand if you wanted to make cookies a different size at home.

You can shape any of these cookies using a larger scoop or a smaller scoop, or use a pan to make bar cookies, etc. You can also roll any of the cookie doughs into a cylinder or log in plastic wrap or parchment paper, then refrigerate or freeze and slice and bake to order. Depending on the size and shape you decide on, alter your baking times accordingly: less time for smaller, flatter cookies; more time for larger, taller cookies. Keep in mind that the time and oven temperature listed in each cookie recipe is for our no. 16, 2¾-ounce NSF blue scoop, Milk Bar's cookie size.

tasting for yourself, thinking for yourself

Baking is the ultimate act of nurturing. Yes, precision is key, but so is remembering you are making delicious food for yourself or someone else. Follow each recipe, tasting every step of the way. You have to know what you're making tastes like before and after—know what too little vanilla extract tastes like, what too much flour and baking powder taste like in a cookie dough. That is how I taught myself to bake.

Taste to learn what tastes good to you. Learn how to use sugars, salt, and citrus juices or citric acid to balance flavors in any recipe. Tweak any recipe if you want it sweeter, saltier, or more acidic. I like sharper balances of flavors. Punch-you-in-the-face-type final products. Sugar, salt, and acid are always noticeable in my desserts, but maybe you like a more subtle balance. Know how to adjust our Cereal Milk (page 35) or Pear Sorbet (page 213) to your taste buds.

tempering eggs is a waste of time

I went to culinary school. I understand and respect the method and intention behind tempering, the classic technique used to gently incorporate raw eggs into a warm liquid or sauce. A small amount of warm mixture is whisked into eggs to temper them, or raise their temperature without running the risk of curdling or scrambling them. The warm eggy mixture is then poured into the remaining warm liquid and heated further.

The thing is, I just don't buy it. At least not in my kitchen. If you incorporate enough of the other ingredients in a recipe into the eggs, blend it all immediately into a homogenous mixture, and then heat that mixture all together, you are still changing the eggs' temperature gently. But you're not dirtying additional kitchen equipment while trying to pour hot liquid from a burner into a bowl on your counter and then back again.

Try it my way before you attempt to wrestle the Banana Cream (page 91) or Sweet Corn Cereal Milk "Ice Cream" Pie Filling (page 45) in some old-fashioned sensibility of tempering.

also, sifting is a waste of time

I don't sift flour. I see it as a messy waste of time. Cookies are meant to be rich and dense, so there's no need to worry about deflating the dough when adding the flour. And although mixing cake flour into a batter without sifting does deflate the mixture ever so slightly, we bake buttery, moist American cakes, not touchy angel food cakes or delicate soufflés. So don't waste your time.

the ten-minute creaming process, or why milk bar cookies are so damn good

In order to achieve the improbable crispy-on-the-outside, fudgy-and-slightly-underbaked-in-the-center defining texture of a Milk Bar cookie—defying science and gravity—a serious creaming process is required. I will go so far as to say it is the *most* important step in making a Milk Bar cookie. Mixing the cookie dough is the first thing any of our cooks learn how to do. Everyone thinks they know how to mix a cookie, but I disagree.

The basics are as follows:

- Use a stand mixer with the paddle attachment. Make sure both the bowl and paddle are at room temperature (not hot out of the dishwasher or dishwater).
- Use room-temperature butter (65° to 70°F). Butter that's too warm will make butter soup; butter that's too cold will take twice as long to cream properly.
- Beat the butter and sugar(s) together on medium-high for 2 to 3 minutes. (If the recipe calls for glucose, add it with the butter and sugar.) This dissolves the sugar while incorporating small pockets of air into the mixture. The air pockets develop as the sugar granules cut into the butter. This creaming process seals the hardbody bond between your butter and sugar.
- Use either cold or room-temperature eggs; room-temperature ones will incorporate more quickly.
- Add the eggs one by one, waiting for each one to be incorporated before adding the next. Then paddle on high for 7 to 8 minutes. The eggs help to strengthen and emulsify the bond.

- If the recipe calls for vanilla extract, add it with the eggs.
- If the butter ever begins to separate or turn into soup on you, throw everything into the fridge for 5 minutes, let the butter firm up, and try again.

You can think of this process in terms of how a croissant bakes. Butter is made up of fat, milk solids, and water. As a croissant bakes, the water content in the butter steams the delicate layers of the croissant apart, creating air pockets and a flaky dough. Without the bond between the butter and the flour, there would be no structure to hold the dough around the air pockets.

So works the bond between butter and sugar in the creaming process. The eggs are the insurance for the butter-sugar bond. In the oven, the butter-sugar bond rises and crisps up, rendering the outside of your cookie delicately crunchy in texture. But if creaming is not executed properly, unbound sugars bake into a dense, sandy cookie, where excess butter without a bond and without a home seeps out onto your pan instead of baking into your cookie.

Signs things are going right:

- The butter mixture is a very pale yellow (with a hint of brown if brown sugar is in the mix).
- The mixture has doubled in size and looks like a cloud: puffy and voluminous, with soft peaks.
- The mixture is slightly shiny and homogenous, with just a little grit from the sugar crystals.

Take this process seriously. Magic doesn't just bake itself in an oven. You can certainly make delicious cookies even without a mixer, melting the butter and mixing the dough with a wooden spoon. But not *these* cookies.

the (in)sane milk bar approach to layering a cake

When we first opened Milk Bar, our bare-bones staff of four would stay into the very wee hours of the morning working—knowing good and well we weren't going home at all, except for maybe a shower and a clean change of clothes. We worked as zombies assembling cakes and scaling each layer of each cake to the gram (including the cake soak).

That's how crazy we were, how much we cared, and yet how little we knew about opening and running a bakery. Ol' Marian Mar is a stickler for detail and she'd be damned if a cake filling was off by a gram. So we have all of our cake fillings measured down to the layer, down to the gram.

If you're an incredibly precise individual, power to you, channel some Marian Mar and get your gem scale out. If you're looking for the path of a little more laid-back cake assembly, divide each filling needed by eye (that's how I do it). Each layer cake purposefully has different filling ratios to balance out the different flavors and textures. So keep that in mind as you go.

making brown butter in the microwave

Know it. Love it. Brown butter is one of the most delicious things to use in any recipe to deepen an already nutty, cinnamony, or brown-sugary flavor. The easiest way to make brown butter at home is in the microwave. Browning the butter in a saucepan on the stove makes you far more likely to burn yourself, or curse like a sailor while trying to scrub the bottom of a saucepan rich in burnt butter solids.

Put the butter in a microwave-safe (Pyrex) bowl, cover the bowl with a microwave-safe saucer or plate, and microwave on high for 3 to 5 minutes,

depending on the amount of butter and heat/intensity of your microwave and its settings. The butter will melt, then start to pop and begin to brown during this period. Don't be shy about browning the butter. You want it deep brown in color and super-nutty in aroma. The lighter in color, the lighter in flavor it will be in the pie, and vice versa—so get it as dark as possible. Cool it completely, stirring it as it cools to distribute the caramelized milk solids evenly.

save your scraps!

Bits and pieces of crumbs, crunches, and fillings make a delicious snack or informal dessert. Helen Jo, one of the chefs who runs Milk Bar, is an artiste when it comes to turning scraps into snacks. She will make you a pint container filled with leftover bits and pieces of recipes piled high into a trifle or just tossed around like a snack mix. She will label the container with your name and draw a hilarious caricature of you (or a dog or a koala bear) before delivery. And not only is the concoction always delicious, it makes you feel like the most important person in the world, or at least the most beloved.

Cake scraps are great as cake truffles (see page 122), but they aren't the only binder for a round snack cluster. Leftover Ritz Crunch (page 53) is amazing when mixed with some Pumpkin Ganache (page 208) and charred marshmallows (page 142). Chocolate crumbs make an amazing salty-sweet Rice Krispie–like treat when you mix it with some leftover mini marshmallows, melted down with butter and Fudge Sauce (page 136).

We also use our leftovers in ice cream recipes or as ice cream toppings.

amazon.com, be forever mine

When I'm baking at home and don't have the amazing wealth of purveyors

carting in daily deliveries of Valrhona chocolate or glucose syrup or freeze-dried corn, I go to the best place for one-stop shopping: amazon.com. They have everything we use in our kitchen, specialty and pedestrian alike, and they'll get it to your doorstep in no time at all. Though I love to go to the grocery store to shop, I abhor bounding from store to store in search of what I need. Which is why, when I need to reup our supply of 6-inch cake rings and acetate, buy some citric acid, or get some candy corn for Halloween flair or a dolphin piñata for Courtney's upcoming birthday—all in 5 minutes— I proudly purr, "Amazon.com, be forever mine."

the tender art of quenelling

I'm not talking about salty creamed whitefish. I'm talking about the shape of that famous French salty, creamy whitefish, or the fancy technique of scooping ice cream into perfect little egg-like forms.

They kind of teach you how to quenelle at culinary school, but almost every savory and pastry cook learns how to quenelle at that first real restaurant job—knee-deep in the middle of dinner service with a sous-chef breathing down your back, taking lopsided excuses for a quenelle and throwing them into the trash, and screaming at you to get your ass in gear. Basically you teach yourself. But I'll try to teach you here.

I do have to say first that by no means does pear sorbet in a quenelle shape taste better than a good old-fashioned sphere of sorbet out of an ice cream scoop. But it is a pretty cool hardbody technique to master:

- You need a well-shaped spoon (choose one that looks most like half an egg), a cup of just barely warm water, and an ice cream (or sorbet) that is neither too hard (temper it in your refrigerator) nor too soft (leave it in your freezer for another hour).

- Dip your spoon into the warm water, insert it into the middle of the ice cream, and pull the spoon toward you until the spoon fills with ice cream.
- If you're right-handed, turn your wrist a quarter to the right, then three-quarters to the left, and finally upward toward the lip of the container of ice cream (see page 131).
- Use the lip of the container to shave off any excess ice cream.
- Warm the bottom of the spoon in your palm. The heat from your hand and the friction against the bottom of the spoon should create just enough heat to release the quenelle.
- Transfer the quenelle to your crumb or crunch or schmear, the nest for your fancy egg-shaped ice cream.

It's an awkward motion that can only be perfected with practice. I don't care how skilled you are: if you've never done it before, you're not going to get it the first time. But keep at it, and you'll get it, I promise.

blooming gelatin: get it right, or do it twice
In order to incorporate it seamlessly into a mixture, gelatin must be softened, or "bloomed," first. To bloom any amount of sheet gelatin, soak it in a small bowl of cold water. The gelatin is bloomed when it has become soft, after about 2 minutes. If the gelatin still has hard bits to it, it needs to bloom longer. If it is so soft it is falling apart, it is overbloomed; discard the gelatin and start over. Gently squeeze the bloomed gelatin to remove any excess water before using.

To bloom powdered gelatin (any amount between ½ teaspoon and 2 teaspoons), sprinkle it evenly onto the surface of 2 tablespoons of cold water in a small cup. If you pour the powdered gelatin into a pile on top of the water, the granules in the center will remain hard and will not bloom. If you use too much water to bloom the gelatin, it will dilute the flavor of the recipe and its consistency will be looser than intended. Allow the granules to soften entirely in the cold water for 3 to 5 minutes.

Once it is bloomed, in order to incorporate either kind of gelatin into a mixture, you need to dissolve the gelatin in hot, but not boiling, liquid—usually a bit of whatever it will be mixed into. If the gelatin gets too hot, it will lose its strength and you will have to start over again.

why the hell is there gelatin in your ice cream base?
We do not use eggs in our ice cream bases unless we are making a brownie ice cream and it needs eggs for flavor. Cereal milk ice cream shouldn't taste eggy, so we don't put eggs in it. We outsmart the traditional approach to making ice cream (which includes tempering eggs and making an egg-milk mixture, called an *anglaise,* that thickens as it heats) by using gelatin as an ice cream stabilizer. It thickens the ice cream, gives it great body and mouth feel— free of crystallization—and keeps it from melting too quickly when you are scooping a sundae or from freezing too hard once stored in the freezer overnight.

wait to spin your ice cream until you are ready to serve it
There is nothing quite like freshly spun (frozen) ice cream. It's the perfect temperature and consistency right out of the ice cream maker. It's

easy to scoop or quenelle and it melts in your mouth just right. In the restaurant industry, when you work in joints that give a damn, you spin the ice creams fresh daily and melt down any leftover ice cream in the fridge each night to "spin" the next day. Apply the same philosophy in your kitchen. Freshly spun ice cream will make you and your friends and family ice cream snobs in all the right ways.

the highbrow "schmear"
This is the fancy sauce presentation you see more and more in dessert (and savory) dishes. It is a step up from the squeeze-bottle dollop or lattice of sauces and dressings.

More or less: you plop a sauce onto one side of a serving plate or bowl. Using the back of a spoon or an offset spatula, in one motion only, apply moderate force and drag the sauce to the fade-out spot at the other end of the plate; ease up on the amount of pressure you are putting on the spoon or spatula as you pull and run out of sauce to drag.

cereal milk™

Cereal milk is my homage to steeped milk.

When I worked at wd~50, we played around infusing milk with all kinds of ingredients—grains, spices, just about anything. Some combinations worked better than others. Some were good, like sesame ice cream, oat panna cotta, and rice sorbet. Some were epic, like toast ice cream: imagine a perfect piece of diner toast—golden brown, crisp (but not so crisp it scrapes the roof of your mouth), saturated in lightly salted butter— and now imagine that as an ice cream flavor.

Cereal milk, by comparison, seems almost dumb. Anyone who's ever spent a lazy Saturday morning, drowning in holey sweatpants, watching hour after hour of USA reruns, knows the flavor: it's that dense, tasty, slightly sweet, kind of starchy, corny milk from the bottom of the cereal bowl.

The seed for it was planted when I was a pastry cook for Wylie and Sam. We were preparing for our spring-to-summer menu changeover, and Sam had cornbread ice cream on the mind. I probably made ten different versions of homemade cornbread, but we couldn't get the corny flavor and guilty pleasure of piping-hot-out-of-the-oven-Jiffy-cornbread just right with my homemade versions. What we got instead were a lot of infused milk tests that all tasted like lame versions of cereal: one tasted like Kix, one like Corn Pops, one like Rice Krispies, one like Special K. They weren't what we were looking for. But, for whatever reason, I felt like I'd learned a secret: milk infusions could hit as close to home as the bottom of my cereal bowl and I happily gulped each failed cornbread milk turned cereal-flavored milk. I filed the idea away deep in the vault and got back to work.

The idea resurfaced when we were opening Ko and our dessert menu had nothing on it. And the new freezer that was supposed to hold the ice cream for that nonexistent dessert menu was on the fritz. The hype was unbearable, and I was screwed. I needed a dessert, period; a backup dessert would be nice too. And if I was smart about it, it would be one that didn't need to be frozen to be good: panna cotta fit that bill perfectly. Now, making a good panna cotta—creamy, set just enough to hold its shape but melt in your mouth—is pretty easy. But making an *interesting* panna cotta—that's the hard part.

The main dessert I was trying to finalize at the time was a deep-fried apple pie—familiar and comforting. Only my initial recipe testing didn't go so well, and seemed rather bleak. I needed a plan in case the apple pie and sour cream ice cream I promised crashed and burned, or the freezer decided not to freeze.

I knew what I had to do: use the familiar and comforting approach, and get smart. I had been training for this moment for years: do a milk infusion. I ran to the 24-hour bodega, bought every powdered and dried thing they had, and made a bunch of adventurous, nasty milk-infused flavors; I gave the cereal milk idea a shot too.

Elsewhere in this book: See other examples of steeped milk in the Pretzel Ice Cream (page 61), the Graham Ice Cream (page 113) and the Saltine Panna Cotta (page 191).

Bulls-eye. Everybody loved it, everybody knew it, nobody saw it coming. The funny part is we worked backward from there. My intention was only to make a cereal milk panna cotta for Ko. But Dave saw something in it, saw the reactions of those who ate it night in and night out. Pushy, pushy man that he is, with the strange soothsayer abilities that he has, Dave forcefully reminded me on many occasions that I should, at the very least, make cereal milk into ice cream. We simplified it even further, too, to create a line of flavored cereal milk to sell at Milk Bar. We make our OG cereal milk with classy old cornflakes, but we've also been known to steep Fruity Pebbles, Cap'n Crunch, and Lucky Charms (the more sugary cereals are what fueled my teenage years and fed my empty stomach, before or after a swig of Diet Mountain Dew—gross but true).

Regardless of whether cereal milk is the beverage for you, the technique— steeping and seasoning milk, then using that milk to make desserts—is a versatile one that exists in pastry and savory kitchens all over the world. It's a technique that's simple and totally accessible in your own home kitchen as well.

cereal milk™

This was by no means the first recipe that came out of our kitchens, but it is far and away the most popular and what we are known best for. Drink it straight, pour it over more cereal, add it to your coffee in the morning, or turn it into panna cotta or ice cream. Cereal milk. It's a way of life.

100 g	cornflakes	2¾ cups
825 g	cold milk	3¾ cups
30 g	light brown sugar	2 tablespoons tightly packed
1 g	kosher salt	¼ teaspoon

1. Heat the oven to 300°F.

2. Spread the cornflakes on a parchment-lined sheet pan. Bake for 15 minutes, until lightly toasted. Cool completely.

3. Transfer the cooled cornflakes to a large pitcher. Pour the milk into the pitcher and stir vigorously. Let steep for 20 minutes at room temperature.

4. Strain the mixture through a fine-mesh sieve, collecting the milk in a medium bowl. The milk will drain off quickly at first, then become thicker and starchy toward the end of the straining process. Using the back of a ladle (or your hand), wring the milk out of the cornflakes, but do not force the mushy cornflakes through the sieve. (We compost the cornflake remains or take them home to our dogs!)

5. Whisk the brown sugar and salt into the milk until fully dissolved. Store in a clean pitcher or glass milk jug, refrigerated, for up to 1 week.

Toasting the cornflakes before steeping them deepens the flavor of the milk. Taste your cereal milk after you make it. If you want it a little sweeter, don't be shy; add a little more brown sugar. If you want a more mellow cereal milk, add a splash of fresh milk and a pinch of salt.

fruity cereal milk™

MAKES ABOUT 690 G (3 CUPS); SERVES 4

It's got an endearing pinky-peach color and it makes killer milkshakes.

If you're not into the color of this finished milk, add a few drops of food coloring to make it any fruity color you please.

Follow the recipe for cereal milk, substituting 100 g (2 cups) Fruity Pebbles for the cornflakes; do *not* toast the Fruity Pebbles. After measuring, crush the cereal with your hands to the texture of coarse sand or gravel, then steep the milk.

sweet corn cereal milk™

MAKES ABOUT 565 G (2¼ CUPS); SERVES 3

This mellow-yellow milk is good straight or over cereal, and it's great poured over toasted cornbread. We use it mainly in a filling for an ice cream pie (see page 45).

Follow the recipe for cereal milk, substituting 100 g (2½ cups) Cap'n Crunch for the cornflakes; do *not* toast the Cap'n Crunch. After measuring, crush the cereal with your hands to the texture of coarse sand or gravel, then steep the milk.

cereal milk™ panna cotta

SERVES 4

Generally speaking, you only need two ingredients to make a delicious panna cotta: flavored milk and gelatin. Salt and light brown sugar are added to the cereal milk in this recipe to deepen and sharpen the flavor of the panna cotta.

The secret to a profesh panna cotta is *just* the right amount of gelatin: Just enough to hold it together. As little as possible, so that the second the panna cotta hits your mouth, it transforms into a silky river of flavored cream. So little that you wonder how the dessert held its shape in the first place.

Serve the panna cotta with fresh fruit and/or Cornflake Crunch (page 51). Or layer it with Banana Cream (page 91) and Hazelnut Crunch (page 185).

Powdered gelatin can be substituted for the sheet gelatin: use ¾ teaspoon.

1½	gelatin sheets	
½ recipe	Cereal Milk (page 35)	320 g (1¼ cups)
25 g	light brown sugar	1½ tablespoons tightly packed
1 g	kosher salt	¼ teaspoon

1. Bloom the gelatin (see page 29).

2. Warm a little bit of the cereal milk and whisk in the gelatin to dissolve. Whisk in the remaining cereal milk, brown sugar, and salt until everything is dissolved, being careful not to incorporate too much air into the mixture.

3. Put 4 small glasses on a flat, transportable surface. Pour the cereal milk mixture into the glasses, filling them equally. Transfer to the refrigerator to set for at least 3 hours, or overnight.

cereal milk™ ice cream

MAKES ABOUT 800 G (1 QUART)

Cereal milk is made. Panna cotta, conquered. Easy, right? On to ice cream.

Scoop the ice cream into your favorite pie crust (see page 59 for our Cereal Milk Ice Cream Pie), sandwich it between your favorite cookies (mine is the Cornflake-Chocolate-Chip-Marshmallow Cookie, page 55), or scoop it into a bowl and decorate with your favorite breakfast cereal and jam or jelly.

Powdered gelatin can be substituted for the sheet gelatin: use ¾ teaspoon. In a pinch, substitute 18 g (1 tablespoon) corn syrup for the glucose.

Instead of a whisk, use a hand blender to mix the ice cream base.

1½	gelatin sheets	
1 recipe	Cereal Milk (page 35)	
4 g	freeze-dried corn powder (see page 18)	2 teaspoons
30 g	light brown sugar	2 tablespoons tightly packed
1 g	kosher salt	¼ teaspoon
20 g	milk powder	¼ cup
50 g	glucose	2 tablespoons

1. Bloom the gelatin (see page 29).

2. Warm a little bit of the cereal milk and whisk in the gelatin to dissolve. Whisk in the remaining cereal milk, the corn powder, brown sugar, salt, milk powder, and glucose until everything is fully dissolved and incorporated.

3. Pour the mixture through a fine-mesh sieve into your ice cream machine and freeze according to the manufacturer's instructions. The ice cream is best spun just before serving or using, but it will keep in an airtight container in the freezer for up to 2 weeks.

fruity cereal milk™ ice cream

MAKES ABOUT 800 G (1 QUART)

Like the original, fruity cereal milk ice cream can be used to fill any of the pie crusts in this book or in a milkshake (fruity cereal milk blended with fruity cereal milk ice cream will change your life). We like it best straight out of the freezer, or scattered with Fruity Pebble Crunch (page 52) on top.

1	gelatin sheet	
1 recipe	Fruity Cereal Milk (page 36)	
130 g	sugar	⅔ cup
2 g	kosher salt	½ teaspoon
20 g	milk powder	¼ cup
50 g	glucose	2 tablespoons

Powdered gelatin can be substituted for the sheet gelatin: use ½ teaspoon. In a pinch, substitute 18 g (1 tablespoon) corn syrup for the glucose.

Instead of a whisk, use a hand blender to mix the ice cream base.

1. Bloom the gelatin (see page 29).

2. Warm a little bit of the fruity cereal milk and whisk in the gelatin to dissolve. Whisk in the remaining fruity cereal milk, the sugar, salt, milk powder, and glucose until everything is fully dissolved and incorporated.

3. Pour the mixture through a fine-mesh sieve into your ice cream machine and freeze according to the manufacturer's instructions. The ice cream is best spun just before serving or using, but it will keep in an airtight container in the freezer for up to 2 weeks.

cereal milk™ white ruskie

SERVES 2

We use the cereal milk ice cream base (the unfrozen ice cream; stop after step 2 in the ice cream recipe) to make white Russians because it stands up to the Kahlúa and vodka better than regular cereal milk does. The liquor in this recipe dulls the cereal milk flavor, so we add freeze-dried corn powder to bring it back.

Why Ruskies? Because I have a younger sister from Kazakhstan and a younger brother from Russia, whom my family affectionately called our "little Ruskies" when they were kids. Here's to Zha-Zha and Dima.

When we make these with frozen ice cream, we call them fancy shakes™. We sell them at Milk Bar and they kill it, every night.

¼ recipe	Cereal Milk Ice Cream base (page 38); not frozen	200 g (1 cup)
4 g	freeze-dried corn powder (see page 18)	2 teaspoons
42 g	Kahlúa	3 tablespoons
42 g	vodka	3 tablespoons

You don't have to be a mixologist to bang this girl out. Whisk together the ice cream base, corn powder, Kahlúa, and vodka in a small pitcher or bowl. Pour into two ice-filled glasses. Or, if you've got the mixology gear, pour into a cocktail shaker filled with ice, cover, and shake until the shaker is frosty. Strain into two old-fashioned glasses filled with ice.

sweet corn cereal milk™ ice cream pie

MAKES 1 (10–INCH) PIE; SERVES 8 TO 10

One summer we had the idea of putting a frozen ice cream pie on the menu at Ssäm Bar. It would be sliced and stored in the freezer, so all the cooks had to do was get it on a plate, put some fruit on top of it, and—booya!—send it out to the table. Not a lot of work for the already-slammed savory cook.

But that was during the time when we were operating out of a portion of the tiny, tiny basement at Ko, and there wasn't any extra real estate for a professional ice cream machine. So we took a little time to think about how we could cheat the process a little—basically, we needed to get rid of the churning while freezing.

We ended up finding that our sweet corn cereal milk was the milk that took to the task the best—the freeze-dried corn and Cap'n Crunch combo has this intense corn pudding flavor. It's so tasty it can be diluted with a lot of fatty, bland cream and still pack a punch of corn flavor. The high proportion of cream, fortified with the starch from the cereal and corn, creates an "ice cream" that freezes soft but hard, a texture kind of like Häagen-Dazs.

Because it gets loose and pourable as it defrosts, the "ice cream" is best for molded frozen uses, like this ice cream pie, or poured into, say, Popsicle molds to make ice cream pops.

Once we had this crazy intense corn ice cream, we set to making a crust corny enough to match it. That process led us down the road to developing our corn cookie, which is the sleeper of all the Milk Bar cookies. It looks so harmless, so plain, so yellow, so un-cookie-like. It's also my grandma's favorite. Her house is surrounded by cornfields, so she's my authority.

225 g	Corn Cookies (recipe follows)	about 3 cookies
25 g	butter, melted, or as needed	2 tablespoons
1 recipe	Sweet Corn Cereal Milk "Ice Cream" Filling (recipe follows)	

1. Put the corn cookies in the food processor and pulse it on and off until the cookies are crumbled into bright yellow sand. (If you don't have a food

Garnish slices of the pie with local fruit of the season. At Ssäm Bar, we macerate a pint of fresh Tristar strawberries (page 214) with a tablespoon of sugar, a very tiny pinch of salt, and ½ teaspoon rice wine vinegar and spoon over the pie slices.

recipe continues

processor, you can fake it till you make it and crumble the corn cookies diligently with your hands into a bowl.)

2. In a bowl, knead the butter and ground cookie mixture by hand until it is moist enough to form a ball. If it is not moist enough to do so, melt an additional 14 g (1 tablespoon) butter and knead it in.

3. Using your fingers and the palms of your hands, press the corn cookie crust firmly into a 10-inch pie plate. Make sure the bottom and the walls of the pie plate are evenly covered. Wrapped in plastic, the crust can be frozen for up to 2 weeks.

4. Use a spatula to scrape and spread the cereal milk "ice cream" filling into the pie shell. Tap the filled pie against the surface of the counter to even the filling. Freeze the pie for at least 3 hours, or until the "ice cream" is frozen and set hard enough to cut and serve. If you're saving your slices of heaven for later, you can freeze the ice cream pie, wrapped in plastic, for up to 2 weeks.

corn cookies

MAKES 13 TO 15 COOKIES

For years, this was a recipe I didn't let out of my kitchen—I don't know why, but everybody has one or two recipes like that. I finally relented and gave a copy to Rick Bishop, Milk Bar's favorite strawberry farmer, and he told me he hid it under his kitchen sink, where he knew it would be safe.

We use corn flour in the corn cookies to deepen the flavor. If you can't find corn flour, you can substitute 40 g (¼ cup) flour and 8 g (4 teaspoons) freeze-dried corn powder (see page 18).

225 g	butter, at room temperature	16 tablespoons (2 sticks)
300 g	sugar	1½ cups
1	egg	
225 g	flour	1⅓ cups
45 g	corn flour	¼ cup
65 g	freeze-dried corn powder (see page 18)	⅔ cup
3 g	baking powder	¾ teaspoon
1.5 g	baking soda	¼ teaspoon
6 g	kosher salt	1½ teaspoons

1. Combine the butter and sugar in the bowl of a stand mixer fitted with the paddle attachment and cream together on medium-high for 2 to 3 minutes. Scrape down the sides of the bowl, add the egg, and beat for 7 to 8 minutes. (See page 27 for notes on this process.)

2. Reduce the mixer speed to low and add the flour, corn flour, corn powder, baking powder, baking soda, and salt. Mix just until the dough comes together, no longer than 1 minute. Scrape down the sides of the bowl.

3. Using a 2¾-ounce ice cream scoop (or a ⅓-cup measure), portion out the dough onto a parchment-lined sheet pan. Pat the tops of the cookie dough domes flat. Wrap the sheet pan tightly in plastic wrap and refrigerate for at least 1 hour, or up to 1 week. Do *not* bake your cookies from room temperature—they will not bake properly.

4. Heat the oven to 350°F.

5. Arrange the chilled dough a minimum of 4 inches apart on parchment- or Silpat-lined sheet pans. Bake for 18 minutes. The cookies will puff, crackle, and spread. After 18 minutes, they should be faintly browned on the edges yet still bright yellow in the center; give them an extra minute if not.

6. Cool the cookies completely on the sheet pans before transferring to a plate or to an airtight container for storage. At room temp, the cookies will keep fresh for 5 days; in the freezer, they will keep for 1 month.

sweet corn cereal milk™ "ice cream" filling

MAKES ENOUGH FILLING FOR 1 SWEET CORN CEREAL MILK ICE CREAM PIE
OR 6 TO 8 POPSICLES

15 g	Cap'n Crunch	¼ cup
25 g	light brown sugar	1½ tablespoons tightly packed
12 g	granulated sugar	1 tablespoon
12 g	freeze-dried corn powder (see page 18)	2 tablespoons
2 g	cornstarch	½ teaspoon
1 g	kosher salt	¼ teaspoon
⅓ recipe	Sweet Corn Cereal Milk (page 36)	175 g (¾ cup)
1	egg	
210 g	heavy cream	1 cup
70 g	sour cream	¼ cup

1. Grind the Cap'n Crunch to a powder in a food processor.

2. Transfer the cereal powder to a large saucepan and add the brown sugar, granulated sugar, corn powder, cornstarch, and salt. Whisk in the cereal milk and egg in a slow, steady stream, whisking until the mixture is clump-free.

3. Put the saucepan over medium-low heat and whisk casually but consistently, watching for the mixture to bubble and thicken, until it has the texture of a pudding or pastry cream—3 to 5 minutes. Scrape the mixture into a small bowl and transfer it to the fridge to cool for 1 hour (you don't want the mixture to firm up completely).

4. Combine the heavy cream and sour cream in the bowl of a stand mixer fitted with the whisk attachment and whip to soft peaks that hold a shape, but just barely. Do not overwhip.

5. Grab the bowl of slightly cooled corn pudding mixture and whisk it into the whipped cream, mixing it for 30 to 45 seconds, until it is a homogenous, slightly runny, totally corny whipped cream delight ready to be poured into a pie shell or Popsicle molds.

milk thistle

is a little farm in upstate New York—Ghent to be exact, just a 2.32-hour minibus ride away from our kitchen—where five of our favorite people and sixty of our favorite cows live. Dante and Kristin Hesse, along with their three children and extended friends and family, care for, corral, and milk their herd of fussy yet endearing Jersey and Holstein cows, all of whom the Hesses know by name and sometimes speak to like unyielding nieces, nephews, aunts, or uncles.

The cows feed on as many natural pastures and as much homegrown hay as possible, though in dire straits and droughts, Dante will feed them a mix of soybeans and corn. The milk is organic and pasteurized but not homogenized, so it has a generous layer of cream on top and real flavor—that of fresh fields and pastures, mostly. I tasted milk from every local producer in the tristate area, and Milk Thistle was my favorite.

My pop worked for the U.S. Department of Agriculture's dairy division for twenty-six years, fighting for small local farmers, writing court decisions, and making sure the big conglomerate organic dairy farmers (whose milk makes us yuppies feel better about ourselves, though the milk has no story, soul, or flavor and very little distinction) don't suffocate heroes like the Hesses.

Dante bet on his love of the land, his cattle, and the art of making milk. He took out a loan and worked day and night to grow his dream, and he's making it. Little by little. Just like us. We support one another, and we know that so much of our success is due to the hard work and dedication out in the fields and pastures of Milk Thistle Farm in Columbia County.

We closed down our kitchen one day this past summer, and went to see where the darling jugs of impossibly creamy and flavorful milk came from. We left with a deeper understanding of how to smile when it rains, the knowledge that skinned knees are as badass as sheet-pan burns, and a line drive to our hearts as a reminder that each jug of milk is made by a small family with skill, thought, and drive. Every drop of milk counts on that farm. The pigs and chickens are fed any leftover milk; a jug sold is part of a loan payment or a piece of used farm equipment to help expedite the milking and pasteurization process. Each jug, therefore, must count in our kitchen. We are a kindred family that survives, fortunately, by doing what we love.

the crunch

Unfortunately, cookie dough is not my only vice.

Sour cream and onion potato chips (the whole bag, in one sitting), sugary cereal by the handful, Cool Ranch Doritos (again, the whole bag, destroyed), crackers dipped in frosting, pretzels dipped in chocolate—you name the snack food—chances are it's gone if I'm standing in the same room with it.

When building a dessert program, I knew part of my voice as a pastry chef, part of what would be lying around the kitchen, and part of what I'd naturally draw inspiration from, would be snack food. Everyone loves snack food. (Or at least everyone who works at Milk Bar.)

The crunch is all about filtering our snacking spells through our formal educations, making crunchy, textural elements all our own. Never too far from the familiar cornflake, pretzel, or cracker, we'll make crunch out of almost anything the supermarket sells and then use it in something as fancy as a plated dessert or as simple as a cookie dough.

Each crunch recipe has a balance of salt and sugar as well as melted butter—the glue for the dry ingredients—and milk powder, which seasons and helps bind the mixture together once baked. The beauty of the crunch, besides the obvious sugar, butter, and snack-attack allure, is the way it's baked. Slow and low in the oven yields the most amazing tender caramelization in every crunchy, snack-ridden handful, cookie, pie crust, or garnish.

cornflake crunch

MAKES ABOUT 360 G (4 CUPS)

This recipe was originally created to accompany the Cereal Milk Panna Cotta (page 37). It was one of those first-swing, home-run hits. It is incredibly simple to make and equally as versatile in its uses. Put some in a plastic bag and take it on the go as the best snack ever, or use it as an ingredient in the recipes that follow.

170 g	cornflakes	½ (12-ounce) box (5 cups)
40 g	milk powder	½ cup
40 g	sugar	3 tablespoons
4 g	kosher salt	1 teaspoon
130 g	butter, melted	9 tablespoons

1. Heat the oven to 275°F.

2. Pour the cornflakes in a medium bowl and crush them with your hands to one-quarter of their original size. Add the milk powder, sugar, and salt and toss to mix. Add the butter and toss to coat. As you toss, the butter will act as glue, binding the dry ingredients to the cereal and creating small clusters.

3. Spread the clusters on a parchment- or Silpat-lined sheet pan and bake for 20 minutes, at which point they should look toasted, smell buttery, and crunch gently when cooled slightly and chewed.

Elsewhere in this book: Cornflake crunch is also used in the Pumpkin Ganache dessert (page 213).

4. Cool the cornflake crunch completely before storing or using in a recipe. Stored in an airtight container at room temperature, the crunch will keep fresh for 1 week; in the fridge or freezer, it will keep for 1 month.

fruity pebble crunch

MAKES ABOUT 225 G (3 CUPS)

Any cereal will yield a delicious crunch. This recipe is a great example of different salt and sugar ratios from the cornflake crunch recipe, because Fruity Pebbles are sweeter. Knowing the sweetness and salt level of the cereal will help you adjust your sugar and salt amounts accordingly when making a crunch out of it.

120 g	Fruity Pebbles	¼ (17-ounce) box (2½ cups)
20 g	milk powder	¼ cup
12 g	sugar	1 tablespoon
1 g	kosher salt	¼ teaspoon
85 g	butter, melted	6 tablespoons

Follow the procedure for the cornflake crunch, substituting the Fruity Pebbles for the cornflakes.

pretzel crunch

MAKES ABOUT 250 G (2 CUPS)

Because so many of our desserts for the restaurants are plated and served by a surly kitchen of 99.9 percent men, we wanted to come up with a deep, malted, surly crunch. This pretzel crunch straddles the line between savory and sweet. Toss this into some Chex Mix on Super Bowl Sunday, or serve it solo in a bowl at your next cocktail party.

100 g	mini pretzels	about ¼ (16-ounce) bag (2 cups)
60 g	light brown sugar	¼ cup tightly packed
25 g	sugar	2 tablespoons
20 g	milk powder	¼ cup
10 g	malt powder	1 tablespoon
100 g	butter, melted	7 tablespoons

In a pinch, substitute flour for malt powder, but part of the malty depth will be lost.

Follow the procedure for the cornflake crunch, substituting the pretzels for the cornflakes and adding the malt powder along with the sugar and milk powder.

ritz crunch

MAKES ABOUT 275 G (2 CUPS)

Any sort of cracker will work here if you adjust the sugar and salt slightly (like for the cereal crunch recipes), but Ritz crackers are the epitome of rich and amazing in my cracker repertoire.

110 g	Ritz crackers	1 sleeve
100 g	sugar	½ cup
20 g	milk powder	¼ cup
2 g	kosher salt	½ teaspoon
100 g	butter, melted	7 tablespoons

Elsewhere in this book: Ritz crunch is used in the Celery Root Ganache dessert (page 214).

Follow the procedure for the cornflake crunch, substituting the crackers for the cornflakes.

cinnamon toast crunch

MAKES ABOUT 250 G (2 CUPS)

The cereal of the same name is excellent stuff, but this recipe is an homage to the cinnamon toast my grandma and ma made me as an after-school snack in my younger years. It is impossibly crunchy, and it plays into one of my most comforting flavor pairings: butter and cinnamon sugar. The one-minute butter-soaking step makes for a much different crunch than the others in this book.

100 g	white sandwich bread	¼ (1-pound) loaf
115 g	brown butter (see page 28), just warm	⅓ cup
100 g	sugar	½ cup
2 g	kosher salt	½ teaspoon
2 g	ground cinnamon	1 teaspoon

1. Heat the oven to 325°F.

2. Tear the bread into ½-inch pieces. Put it in a bowl, then douse and toss it with the brown butter. Let the bread soak for 1 minute.

3. Add the sugar, salt, and cinnamon to the bread and toss well. Spread the mixture on a parchment- or Silpat-lined sheet pan and bake for 25 minutes.

4. Pull the sheet pan slightly out of the oven and, using a spatula, a spoon, or whatever you've got, break up the cinnamon toast crunch a bit and toss it around, to make sure it is caramelizing and drying out. Bake for an additional 5 minutes or more, until you have dry, caramelized clusters.

5. Cool the cinnamon toast crunch completely before storing or using in a recipe. Stored in an airtight container at room temperature, it will keep fresh for 1 week; in the fridge or freezer, it will keep for 1 month.

cornflake-chocolate-chip-marshmallow cookies

MAKES 15 TO 20 COOKIES

I am neither brave nor bold enough to make *just* a chocolate chip cookie. Everyone's mom or grandma makes "the best" chocolate chip cookie. And every one of those chocolate chip cookie recipes is different. So, out of respect, we dared not compete. Instead, we made a delicious chocolate chip tribute cookie—one of our most popular cookies—by accident.

In the Ko basement one day, Mar overtoasted the cornflake crunch for the cereal milk panna cotta. She was pissed. I was pissed. But we refused to let it go to waste. I was already well versed in making a cookie out of anything left in the pantry, and we needed a dessert for family meal anyway. So we made cookies with the cornflake crunch, and we threw in some mini chocolate chips, just to make them appealing to the cooks in case the overtoasted cornflakes were a bust, and some mini marshmallows, because we were eating them as a snack, and why the hell not. It was just family meal.

The cooks freaked. They requested the cookies for family meal every day after that. And so the cornflake-chocolate-chip-marshmallow cookie was born—love at first bite and a shoo-in on Milk Bar's opening menu.

225 g	butter, at room temperature	16 tablespoons (2 sticks)
250 g	granulated sugar	1¼ cups
150 g	light brown sugar	⅔ cup tightly packed
1	egg	
2 g	vanilla extract	½ teaspoon
240 g	flour	1½ cups
2 g	baking powder	½ teaspoon
1.5 g	baking soda	¼ teaspoon
5 g	kosher salt	1¼ teaspoons
¾ recipe	Cornflake Crunch (page 51)	270 g (3 cups)
125 g	mini chocolate chips	⅔ cup
65 g	mini marshmallows	1¼ cups

recipe continues

1. Combine the butter and sugars in the bowl of a stand mixer fitted with the paddle attachment and cream together on medium-high for 2 to 3 minutes. Scrape down the sides of the bowl, add the egg and vanilla, and beat for 7 to 8 minutes. (See page 27 for notes on this process.)

2. Reduce the mixer speed to low and add the flour, baking powder, baking soda, and salt. Mix just until the dough comes together, no longer than 1 minute. (Do not walk away from the machine during this step, or you will risk overmixing the dough.) Scrape down the sides of the bowl with a spatula.

3. Still on low speed, paddle in the cornflake crunch and mini chocolate chips just until they're incorporated, no more than 30 to 45 seconds. Paddle in the mini marshmallows just until incorporated.

4. Using a 2¾-ounce ice cream scoop (or a ⅓-cup measure), portion out the dough onto a parchment-lined sheet pan. Pat the tops of the cookie dough domes flat. Wrap the sheet pan tightly in plastic wrap and refrigerate for at least 1 hour, or up to 1 week. Do *not* bake your cookies from room temperature—they will not hold their shape.

5. Heat the oven to 375°F.

6. Arrange the chilled dough a minimum of 4 inches apart on parchment- or Silpat-lined sheet pans. Bake for 18 minutes. The cookies will puff, crackle, and spread. At the 18-minute mark, the cookies should be browned on the edges and just beginning to brown toward the center. Leave them in the oven for an additional minute or so if they aren't and they still seem pale and doughy on the surface.

7. Cool the cookies completely on the sheet pans before transferring to a plate or to an airtight container for storage. At room temperature, the cookies will keep fresh for 5 days; in the freezer, they will keep for 1 month.

holiday cookies

MAKES 18 TO 22 COOKIES

We're awfully fond of celebrating the holidays with annoying decorative knick-knacks. Or, rather, my mother loves to buy annoying decorative knickknacks and send them to us, and we love to make it look like a holiday just threw up in our kitchen.

We like our cookies to celebrate the holidays too—that's how we came up with our winter "holiday" cookie, a cornflake-marshmallow cookie with crushed candy canes in it.

| 200 g | peppermints or candy canes | 40 peppermints or 18 candy canes |

Unwrap the candy and transfer it to a medium zip-top plastic bag. With the end of a rolling pin, break the candy up into medium to small pieces, at least one quarter in size, no smaller than a Nerd, being careful not to make candy powder. Follow the recipe for cornflake-chocolate-chip-marshmallow cookies, adding the candy pieces with the mini marshmallows.

fruity pebble marshmallow cookies

MAKES 12 TO 17 COOKIES

Follow the recipe for the cornflake-chocolate-chip-marshmallow cookies, substituting Fruity Pebble Crunch (page 52) for the cornflake crunch and omitting the chocolate chips.

cereal milk™ ice cream pie

MAKES 1 (10-INCH) PIE; SERVES 8 TO 10

This was the template, the training-wheels version, for many tasty and elaborate frozen pies that came after it. It's also the easiest, most crowd-pleasing dessert you can make in a jiffy with some cornflakes and mother recipes you have on hand in your kitchen. Decorate the pie with any fruit you like to put in your breakfast cereal (bananas! strawberries! blueberries!).

½ recipe	Cornflake Crunch (page 51)	180 g (2 cups)
25 g	butter, melted	2 tablespoons
1 recipe	Cereal Milk Ice Cream (page 38)	

1. Using your hands (or a food processor if you prefer), crumble the cornflake crunch clusters to half their size. (The smaller size will make for better distribution of the moisture and fat, creating a nice crunchy crust.)

2. Toss the melted butter into the crumbled cornflake crunch, mixing well. Using your fingers and the palms of your hands, press the mixture firmly into a 10-inch pie tin, making sure the bottom and sides of the pie tin are evenly covered. Wrapped in plastic, the crust can be frozen for up to 2 weeks.

3. Use a spatula to spread the ice cream into the pie shell. Freeze the pie for at least 3 hours, or until the ice cream is frozen hard enough so the pie is easy to cut and serve. Wrapped in plastic wrap, the pie will keep for 2 weeks in the freezer.

pretzel ice cream pie

MAKES 1 (10-INCH) PIE; SERVES 8 TO 10

A deeper, darker, saltier version of the cereal milk ice cream pie—try this one for the salty but sweet fans.

1 recipe	Pretzel Crunch (page 52)	
25 g	butter, melted	2 tablespoons
1 recipe	Pretzel Ice Cream (recipe follows)	

Follow the procedure for the cereal milk ice cream pie, substituting the pretzel crunch for the cornflake crunch and pretzel ice cream for the cereal milk ice cream.

pretzel ice cream

MAKES ABOUT 700 G (1 QUART)

300 g	mini pretzels	about ¾ (16-ounce) bag (6 cups)
440 g	milk	2 cups
1½	gelatin sheets	
200 g	glucose	½ cup
30 g	light brown sugar	2 tablespoons tightly packed
45 g	cream cheese	1½ ounces
2 g	kosher salt	½ teaspoon
0.75 g	baking soda	⅛ teaspoon

Powdered gelatin can be substituted for the sheet gelatin: use ¾ teaspoon. In a pinch, substitute 75 g (¼ cup) corn syrup for the glucose.

This recipe uses cream cheese to give an even creamier texture and mouth feel to the ice cream; it works well because the malty pretzel flavor overpowers the flavor of the cream cheese.

1. Heat the oven to 300°F.

2. Spread the pretzels on a sheet pan and toast for 15 minutes, until the pretzels have slightly darkened in color and your kitchen smells pretzely. Cool completely.

recipe continues

3. Put the pretzels in a large bowl, pour the milk over them, and stir while steeping for 2 minutes.

4. Strain the milk mixture through a fine-mesh sieve and discard the soggy pieces of pretzel.

5. Bloom the gelatin (see page 29).

Instead of a whisk, use a hand blender to mix the ice cream base.

6. Warm a little bit of the pretzel milk and whisk in the gelatin to dissolve. Add the remaining pretzel milk, glucose, brown sugar, cream cheese, salt, and baking soda and whisk until all of the ingredients are fully dissolved and incorporated.

7. Pour the mixture into your ice cream machine and freeze according to the manufacturer's instructions. The ice cream is best spun just before serving or using, but it will keep in an airtight container in the freezer for up to 2 weeks.

pb & j pie

MAKES 1 (10-INCH) PIE; SERVES 8 TO 10

One of the first fall desserts ever put on the menu at Ssäm Bar was a riff on the poor man's pb & j: peanut butter, Concord grape jelly, and a saltine panna cotta (page 191). We loved the Ritz crunch crust so much that the following fall, we presented the pb & j in a more straightforward pie, showcasing Concord grapes in another light, with Ritz crust bringing the same salty, starchy component as the saltine panna cotta.

1 recipe	*unbaked* Ritz Crunch (page 53)
1 recipe	Peanut Butter Nougat (page 178)
1 recipe	Concord Grape Sorbet (recipe follows)
½ recipe	Concord Grape Sauce (recipe follows)

1. Heat the oven to 275°F.

2. Press the Ritz crunch into a 10-inch pie tin. Using your fingers and the palms of your hands, press the crunch in firmly, making sure to cover the bottom and sides evenly and completely.

3. Put the tin on a sheet pan and bake for 20 minutes. The Ritz crust should be slightly more golden brown and slightly deeper in buttery goodness than the crunch you started with. Cool the Ritz crunch crust completely; wrapped in plastic, the crust can be frozen for up to 2 weeks.

4. Scatter the peanut butter nougat over the bottom of the pie crust and then gently press it down to form a flat layer. Freeze this layer for 30 minutes or until cold and firm. Scoop the sorbet onto the nougat and spread it into an even layer. Put the pie in the freezer until the sorbet firms up, 30 minutes to 1 hour.

5. Spoon the Concord grape sauce onto the top of the pie and, working quickly, spread it evenly over the sorbet. Pop the pie back into the freezer until ready to slice and serve. Wrapped (gently) in plastic, the pie can be frozen for up to 1 month.

concord grape juice

MAKES ABOUT 675 G (2½ CUPS)

Concord grapes are one of the greatest things on God's green earth. There really is no substitute for their fresh grapey flavor. Make this juice when the grapes are in season and then freeze it so you never have to live without it.

675 g	Concord grapes, stems left on	2 quarts
220 g	water	1 cup
65 g	sugar	⅓ cup

1. Combine the grapes, water, and sugar in a large heavy-bottomed saucepan and bring to a slow boil, then simmer until the grapes have broken down, about 1 hour. As they cook, gently mash the grapes with a slotted spoon to help them release their juices. Your kitchen will begin to smell like grape-flavored bubble gum: this is a good sign.

Elsewhere in this book: Concord grape juice is used in Concord Grape Jelly (page 190).

2. Once the grapes have surrendered most of their juices and begun to look more like raisins, remove from the heat. Using tongs or a slotted spoon, remove the grape carcasses and transfer to a fine-mesh sieve set over a large bowl. Pour the juice over the grapes and press down on them to get every last bit of juice out of them. (We compost the remaining skins, seeds, and stems.)

3. Use the grape juice right away, or store it in an airtight container in your fridge for up to 1 week or in your freezer for up to 1 year.

concord grape sorbet

MAKES ABOUT 475 G (1 PINT)

1	gelatin sheet	

½ recipe	Concord Grape Juice (opposite)	

200 g	glucose	½ cup
2 g	citric acid (see page 16)	½ teaspoon
1 g	kosher salt	¼ teaspoon

1. Bloom the gelatin (see page 29).

2. Warm a little bit of the grape juice and whisk in the gelatin to dissolve. Whisk in the remaining grape juice, the glucose, citric acid, and salt until everything is fully dissolved and incorporated.

3. Pour the mixture into your ice cream machine and freeze according to the manufacturer's instructions. The sorbet is best spun just before serving or using, but it will keep in an airtight container in the freezer for up to 2 weeks.

With all things fresh and seasonal, it's always important to taste, taste, taste. Make the sorbet base to your liking with more glucose, salt, or citric acid (see page 26).

Powdered gelatin can be substituted for the sheet gelatin: use ½ teaspoon. In a pinch, substitute 75 g (¼ cup) corn syrup for the glucose.

Instead of a whisk, use a hand blender to mix the sorbet base.

concord grape sauce

MAKES ABOUT 360 G (1¼ CUPS)

½ recipe	Concord Grape Juice (opposite)	
14 g	sherry vinegar	1 tablespoon
50 g	sugar	¼ cup
1 g	kosher salt	¼ teaspoon

2	gelatin sheets	

1. Heat half of the grape juice with the vinegar, sugar, and salt in a large heavy-bottomed saucepan, stirring occasionally, until the sugar and salt dissolve. Remove from the heat.

2. Bloom the gelatin (see page 29). Add it to the hot grape juice mixture, whisking to dissolve, then add the remaining grape juice. Cool the sauce partially in the fridge for 30 minutes, so it is still fluid enough to spread atop the pie, or put the sauce in an airtight container and store it in your fridge for up to 2 weeks.

Powdered gelatin can be substituted for the sheet gelatin: use 1 teaspoon.

grapefruit pie

MAKES 1 (10-INCH) PIE; SERVES 8 TO 10

We fell so in love with the Ritz crunch that we decided to start recipe testing a few pie options using it as a crust. As we delved deeper into the world of pies, we became obsessed with both the concept and the technique of Ohio Shaker pie (a traditional Americana pie, where thinly sliced lemons are tenderized without heat in sugar and a little salt) and key lime pie (the South's best use of sweetened condensed milk, which naturally thickens with the acidity of the key lime juice). We tried as many different citrus fruits as possible, thinly sliced and layered with sugar into a pie shell, or juiced and stirred into sweetened condensed milk. Grapefruit was the clear winner, and it turns out that combining the two pie methods made for our favorite recipe—though instead of thinly slicing the grapefruit and candying it, we make grapefruit threads so you get the same tangy grapefruit pop in every bite of pie.

This recipe is a little more involved than others in this chapter, but it's delicious and worth a few more minutes of your time.

1 recipe	*unbaked* Ritz Crunch (page 53)
1 recipe	Grapefruit Passion Curd (recipe follows)
1 recipe	Sweetened Condensed Grapefruit (recipe follows)

1. Heat the oven to 275°F.

2. Press the Ritz crunch into a 10-inch pie tin. Using your fingers and the palms of your hands, press the crunch in firmly, making sure to cover the bottom and sides evenly and completely.

3. Put the tin on a sheet pan and bake for 20 minutes. The Ritz crust should be slightly more golden brown and slightly deeper in buttery goodness than the crunch you started with. Cool the crust completely; wrapped in plastic, the crust can be frozen for up to 2 weeks.

4. Using a spoon or an offset spatula, spread the grapefruit passion curd evenly over the bottom of the Ritz crust. Put the pie in the freezer to set the curd until firm, about 30 minutes.

recipe continues

5. Using a spoon or an offset spatula, spread the sweetened condensed grapefruit on top of the curd, being careful not to mix the two layers and making sure the curd is entirely covered. Return to the freezer until ready to slice and serve. Wrapped (gently) in plastic, the pie can be frozen for up to 1 month.

grapefruit passion curd

MAKES ABOUT 350 G (1¼ CUPS)

Passion fruit puree can be found in Latin grocery stores and online at amazon.com.

50 g	passion fruit puree	¼ cup
40 g	sugar	3 tablespoons
1	egg	
½	gelatin sheet	
85 g	very cold butter	6 tablespoons
1 g	kosher salt	¼ teaspoon
1	large grapefruit	
3 g	grapeseed oil	1 teaspoon

Powdered gelatin can be substituted for the sheet gelatin: use ¼ teaspoon.

1. Put the passion fruit puree and sugar in a blender and blend until the sugar granules have dissolved. Add the egg and blend on low until you have a bright orange-yellow mixture. Transfer the contents of the blender to a medium pot or saucepan. Clean the blender canister.

2. Bloom the gelatin (see page 29).

3. Heat the passion fruit mixture over low heat, whisking regularly. As it heats up, it will begin to thicken; keep a close eye on it. Once the mixture boils, remove it from the stove and transfer it to the blender. Add the bloomed gelatin, butter, and salt and blend until the mixture is thick, shiny, and super-smooth.

4. Transfer the mixture to a heatproof container, and put in the fridge for 30 to 60 minutes, until the passion fruit curd has cooled completely.

5. While the passion fruit curd is cooling, use a paring knife to carefully remove the rind from the grapefruit. Remove every last bit of it—leave no white pith behind! Then carefully remove each segment of grapefruit from its membranes by slicing down both sides of each segment, along the membrane, to the center of the fruit; the segments should come right out. (The technical term for this process is "suprêming" the fruit.)

6. Put the grapefruit segments in a small saucepan with the grapeseed oil and warm over low heat, stirring occasionally and gently with a spoon. After about 2 minutes, the warm oil will help separate and encapsulate the individual grapefruit "threads." Remove from the heat and let the threads cool slightly before proceeding.

7. Using a spoon or rubber spatula, gently stir the grapefruit threads into the cooled passion fruit curd. Use immediately, or transfer to an airtight container and store in the fridge for up to 1 week.

sweetened condensed grapefruit

MAKES ABOUT 275 G (1 CUP)

The acid from the grapefruit juice and citric acid will naturally thicken the sweetened condensed milk, which is one of the coolest things to watch happen right before your very eyes.

225 g	sweetened condensed milk	¾ cup
30 g	Tropicana Ruby Red grapefruit juice	2 tablespoons
2 g	kosher salt	½ teaspoon
2 g	citric acid (see page 16)	½ teaspoon
1 drop	red food coloring	

Combine the sweetened condensed milk, grapefruit juice, salt, citric acid, and food coloring in a medium bowl and mix with a rubber spatula by stirring and folding over the mixture until it is homogenous. Use immediately, or transfer to an airtight container and store in the fridge for up to 2 weeks.

the crumb

"The crumb" is our name for clumpy, crunchy, yet sandy little bits of flavor. I started using the crumb in the fancier plated desserts I made for Ssäm Bar and Ko: put some crumbs under a scoop of ice cream, and it won't slide across the plate before it gets to the guest. Soon enough, leftover crumb made its way into the cookies I baked for family meal, then into birthday cakes, and then it was open season. As a result, almost all of our pie crusts at Milk Bar are based on a crumb that we grind with butter and salt before pressing into a pie tin.

My first face-to-face with the crumb was when I was a pastry cook at wd~50—Sam Mason, the pastry chef, called his crumbs "soils." (Nearly every pastry chef I know has at least one crumb or soil on his or her menu these days.) At wd~50, we made chocolate soil, coffee soil (my favorite), cherry soil, onion soil, pea soil, and on and on. I was so enamored with the soils that I knew I wanted to have my own recipes, flavors, and uses for the technique for the day when I would be in charge of my own kitchen.

The basic technique to make the crumb is this: dehydrate and/or pulverize your flavor base (or use a flavorful dry substance, like cocoa powder or ground coffee); toss it with flour, sugar, and salt to balance the flavor base; bind it together with butter; and bake.

Years later at Milk Bar, I wanted to blow the lid off the crumb world by making crumbs in quirky flavors that no one else had. But I needed to change my approach to the makeup of ingredients and the major flavor bases. See, we'd used blanched almond flour (along with a small amount of regular flour) as the binder at wd~50, but with all the nut allergies we see at the restaurants, I knew the almond flour had to go—which sucked, because it really adds a nice flavor and richness.

I went to my favorite 24-hour bodega down Second Avenue late one night and cleared out the dried and powdered goods selection (a regular routine of mine). I bought a world of powdered everything: honey powder, iced tea powder, Nesquik Strawberry Milk Powder, mustard powder. I walked back into the kitchen and stacked my finds on the dry goods shelf. But though I was sure they would all make interesting crumbs—at least I thought that they all could be really delicious—none struck me with the accessible yet subtle cleverness I wanted to convey. Then, down the kitchen, I spied the milk powder I use to make soft-serve ice cream.

I looked at it sideways, wondered, "What if . . . ?" I went for it. I tossed it with flour, sugar, salt, cornstarch (the binder I decided to use in place of almond flour), and melted butter.

Straight out of the oven, it wasn't exactly the milky flavor I wanted it to be, but it was headed somewhere good. It needed more milkiness. I settled on melted white chocolate as the solution. In addition to elevating the creamy milkiness, white chocolate improved the texture—binding and moistening it, as well as sweetening it further—moving it away from a milk "soil" and toward a milk "crumb."

I know it seems funny for me to say, but I don't drink straight milk and haven't since childhood, when my mom made me. Still, I am in love with the idea of the flavor I *think* milk should have—and these milk crumbs were the first perfect embodiment of that idealized milk flavor. They have a richness, butteriness, and sweetness (from that enrobing with white chocolate) that makes any hater want to love the flavor of milk.

I've come to love the milk crumb because it is an unobvious use for an obvious ingredient. Milk powder is on hand in nearly every professional pastry kitchen and plenty of home cupboards, but nobody takes advantage of its versatility. Our milk crumbs go in cookies, cakes, and pie crusts, and that's just the beginning. With the addition of malt powder, they turn into malted milk crumbs; with instant tea, they take on the flavor of a really milky cup of black tea. Add a little freeze-dried peach powder, and suddenly they're peaches-and-cream-flavored crumbs—and on and on.

There was no push to put "milky" things on the menu; like most successful Momofuku things, it just kind of happened. Milk Bar was already going to be Milk Bar before the milk crumb came into being, but I soon discovered my obsession with exploiting milk, milk crumbs, and cereal milk in a million different ways.

It's the conversation I always have with Dave: the basis of our best dishes is making something out of nothing. I had a bunch of powdered goodness from the deli, but it was the milk powder already sitting in the kitchen that ended up as the catalyst that really sparked me. It's a good challenge to keep in mind: make yourself see the unobvious in things you already have. Find a new use for the same products you use daily. You just have to look at them sideways and wonder, "What if . . . ?"

milk crumb

MAKES ABOUT 260 G (2¼ CUPS)

40 g	milk powder	½ cup
40 g	flour	¼ cup
12 g	cornstarch	2 tablespoons
25 g	sugar	2 tablespoons
2 g	kosher salt	½ teaspoon
55 g	butter, melted	4 tablespoons (½ stick)
20 g	milk powder	¼ cup
90 g	white chocolate, melted	3 ounces

1. Heat the oven to 250°F.

2. Combine the 40 g (½ cup) milk powder, the flour, cornstarch, sugar, and salt in a medium bowl. Toss with your hands to mix. Add the melted butter and toss, using a spatula, until the mixture starts to come together and form small clusters.

3. Spread the clusters on a parchment- or Silpat-lined sheet pan and bake for 20 minutes. The crumbs should be sandy at that point, and your kitchen should smell like buttery heaven. Cool the crumbs completely.

4. Crumble any milk crumb clusters that are larger than ½ inch in diameter, and put the crumbs in a medium bowl. Add the 20 g (¼ cup) milk powder and toss together until it is evenly distributed throughout the mixture.

5. Pour the white chocolate over the crumbs and toss until your clusters are enrobed. Then continue tossing them every 5 minutes until the white chocolate hardens and the clusters are no longer sticky. The crumbs will keep in an airtight container in the fridge or freezer for up to 1 month.

Elsewhere in this book: Milk crumbs are used in the White Peach Sorbet dessert (page 130).

berry milk crumb

MAKES ABOUT 320 G (2½ CUPS)

Freeze-dried fruit! The range of delicious freeze-dried fruits and veggies can make your world of crumb possibilities seem endless. We grind down freeze-dried fruits and veggies into a powder in a blender or food processor and then toss them with milk crumbs to give pops of new flavor to an old crumb. We adjust the moisture with butter or white chocolate if necessary, based on the ingredients in the mix and our end goal.

1 recipe	Milk Crumb (page 74)	
40 g	freeze-dried cherry powder	½ cup
20 g	freeze-dried blueberry powder	¼ cup
0.5 g	kosher salt	⅛ teaspoon

Toss the milk crumbs with the berry powders and salt in a medium bowl until all of the crumbs are an evenly speckled red and blue, coated in the berry powder. The crumbs will keep in an airtight container in the fridge or freezer for up to 1 month.

malted milk crumb

MAKES ABOUT 375 G (2½ CUPS)

1 recipe	Milk Crumb (page 74)	
60 g	Ovaltine, malt flavor	¾ cup
90 g	white chocolate, melted	3 ounces

1. Toss the milk crumbs with the Ovaltine malt powder in a medium bowl until all of the crumbs are a light brown.

Elsewhere in this book: Malted milk crumbs are used in the Chocolate Malt Layer Cake (page 139).

2. Pour the white chocolate over the crumbs and continue tossing until all of the clusters are enrobed. Then continue tossing them every 5 minutes until the white chocolate hardens and the clusters are no longer sticky. (The result will be just like the original milk crumb, but with a cheetah-like spotting of light brown malt powder.) The crumbs will keep in an airtight container in the fridge or freezer for up to 1 month.

chocolate crumb

MAKES ABOUT 350 G (2½ CUPS)

105 g	flour	⅔ cup
4 g	cornstarch	1 teaspoon
100 g	sugar	½ cup
65 g	cocoa powder, preferably Valrhona	⅔ cup
4 g	kosher salt	1 teaspoon
85 g	butter, melted	6 tablespoons

1. Heat the oven to 300°F.

2. Combine the flour, cornstarch, sugar, cocoa powder, and salt in the bowl of a stand mixer fitted with the paddle attachment and paddle on low speed until mixed.

3. Add the butter and paddle on low speed until the mixture starts to come together in small clusters.

4. Spread the clusters on a parchment- or Silpat-lined sheet pan. Bake for 20 minutes, breaking them up occasionally. The crumbs should still be slightly moist to the touch at that point; they will dry and harden as they cool.

5. Let the crumbs cool completely before using in a recipe or eating. Stored in an airtight container, they will keep fresh for 1 week at room temperature or 1 month in the fridge or freezer.

birthday cake crumb

MAKES ABOUT 275 G (2¼ CUPS)

What's better than box cake, you might ask? Nothing, actually. All I really want for breakfast, lunch, or dinner is box cake and its amazing wealth of by-products. I typically allow this 24-hour splurge only on my birthday.

The one thing that always eluded me, though, was how the hell do they get box cake to taste like that?! I have made coffee cake, soup, cookies, clusters, and cereal out of it. So we undertook the recipe development task of re-creating my favorite, and the ultimate birthday box cake, Funfetti, from scratch.

It took us four months to get there. And we still don't make our own rainbow sprinkles (which Wylie Dufresne calls "cheating"). But I couldn't be happier with the results: the crumbs, Birthday Cake (page 105), Birthday Cake Frosting (page 107), and Confetti Cookies (page 100). My dream come true.

100 g	granulated sugar	½ cup
25 g	light brown sugar	1½ tablespoons tightly packed
90 g	cake flour	¾ cup
2 g	baking powder	½ teaspoon
2 g	kosher salt	½ teaspoon
20 g	rainbow sprinkles	2 tablespoons
40 g	grapeseed oil	¼ cup
12 g	*clear* vanilla extract (see page 21)	1 tablespoon

1. Heat the oven to 300°F.

2. Combine the sugars, flour, baking powder, salt, and sprinkles in the bowl of a stand mixer fitted with the paddle attachment and mix on low speed until well combined.

3. Add the oil and vanilla and paddle again to distribute. The wet ingredients will act as glue to help the dry ingredients form small clusters; continue paddling until that happens.

4. Spread the clusters on a parchment- or Silpat-lined sheet pan. Bake for 20 minutes, breaking them up occasionally. The crumbs should still be slightly moist to the touch; they will dry and harden as they cool.

5. Let the crumbs cool completely before using in a recipe or scarfing by the handful. Stored in an airtight container, the crumbs will keep fresh for 1 week at room temperature or 1 month in the fridge or freezer.

pie crumb

MAKES ABOUT 350 G (2¾ CUPS)

These crumbs give all the flavor and none of the fuss of a traditional pie crust.

240 g	flour	1½ cups
18 g	sugar	2 tablespoons
3 g	kosher salt	¾ teaspoon

115 g	butter, melted	8 tablespoons (1 stick)
20 g	water	1½ tablespoons

1. Heat the oven to 350°F.

2. Combine the flour, sugar, and salt in the bowl of a stand mixer fitted with the paddle attachment and paddle on low speed until well mixed.

3. Add the butter and water and paddle on low speed until the mixture starts to come together in small clusters.

4. Spread the clusters on a parchment- or Silpat-lined sheet pan. Bake for 25 minutes, breaking them up occasionally. The crumbs should be golden brown and still slightly moist to the touch at that point; they will dry and harden as they cool.

5. Let the crumbs cool completely before using in a recipe or eating. Stored in an airtight container, the crumbs will keep fresh for 1 week at room temperature or 1 month in the fridge or freezer.

Elsewhere in this book: Pie crumbs are used in the Apple Pie Layer Cake (page 157).

blueberry & cream cookies

MAKES 12 TO 17 COOKIES

After the milk crumb phenomenon in the kitchen, we had to find a mainstream use for it, rather than just hiding it under some ice cream. It needed its moment in the sun. So I brainstormed. A peaches-and-cream cookie was my original thought. *Momofuku* does mean "lucky peach" in Japanese, after all. But I decided we needed something that would hit home even more for guests.

Did you know dried blueberries existed? I didn't, until I surveyed Whole Foods' dried fruit selection for a dried peach alternative. The clouds parted, and it was clear. We needed a blueberry-and-cream cookie, reminiscent of a blueberry muffin top (the best part of the muffin).

You can substitute Berry Milk Crumb (page 75) for the milk crumbs to make the cookies more fruity. In a pinch, substitute 35 g (2 tablespoons) corn syrup for the glucose.

225 g	butter, at room temperature	16 tablespoons (2 sticks)
150 g	granulated sugar	¾ cup
150 g	light brown sugar	⅔ cup tightly packed
100 g	glucose	¼ cup
2	eggs	
320 g	flour	2 cups
2 g	baking powder	½ teaspoon
1.5 g	baking soda	¼ teaspoon
6 g	kosher salt	1½ teaspoons
½ recipe	Milk Crumb (page 74)	
130 g	dried blueberries	¾ cup

1. Combine the butter, sugars, and glucose in the bowl of a stand mixer fitted with the paddle attachment and cream on medium-high for 2 to 3 minutes. Scrape down the sides of the bowl, add the eggs, and beat for 7 to 8 minutes. (See page 27 for notes on this process.)

2. Reduce the mixer speed to low and add the flour, baking powder, baking soda, and salt. Mix just until the dough comes together, no longer than 1 minute. (Do not walk away from the machine during this step, or you will risk overmixing the dough.) Scrape down the sides of the bowl with a spatula.

3. Still on low speed, add the milk crumbs and mix until they're incorporated, no more than 30 seconds. Chase the milk crumbs with the dried blueberries, mixing them in for 30 seconds.

4. Using a 2¾-ounce ice cream scoop (or a ⅓-cup measure), portion out the dough onto a parchment-lined sheet pan. Pat the tops of the cookie dough domes flat. Wrap the sheet pan tightly in plastic wrap and refrigerate for at least 1 hour, or up to 1 week. Do *not* bake your cookies from room temperature—they will not bake properly.

5. Heat the oven to 350°F.

6. Arrange the chilled dough a minimum of 4 inches apart on parchment- or Silpat-lined sheet pans. Bake for 18 minutes. The cookies will puff, crackle, and spread. After 18 minutes, they should be very faintly browned on the edges yet still bright yellow in the center; give them an extra minute or so if that's not the case.

7. Cool the cookies completely on the sheet pans before transferring to a plate or to an airtight container for storage. At room temp, the cookies will keep fresh for 5 days; in the freezer, they will keep for 1 month.

pistachio layer cake

MAKES 1 (6-INCH) LAYER CAKE, 5 TO 6 INCHES TALL; SERVES 6 TO 8

This cake was a bestseller at Milk Bar right off the bat. If you've had it, chances are you were hooked at first bite. Though the recipe calls for a few things that you'll have to source aside from your normal pantry ingredients, remember that amazon.com can be the love of your life too, and that this cake is well worth the effort.

1 recipe	Pistachio Cake (recipe follows)	
65 g	pistachio oil	⅓ cup
1 recipe	Lemon Curd (recipe follows)	
½ recipe	Milk Crumb (page 74)	
1 recipe	Pistachio Frosting (recipe follows)	

Grapeseed oil can be substituted for the pistachio oil, but part of the toasted-pistachio depth of flavor will be lost.

special equipment

1 (6-inch) cake ring

2 strips acetate, each 3 inches wide and 20 inches long

1. Put a piece of parchment or a Silpat on the counter. Invert the cake onto it and peel off the parchment or Silpat from the bottom of the cake. Use the cake ring to stamp out 2 circles from the cake. These are your top 2 cake layers. The remaining cake "scrap" will come together to make the bottom layer of the cake.

layer 1, the bottom

2. Clean the cake ring and place it in the center of a sheet pan lined with clean parchment or a Silpat. Use 1 strip of acetate to line the inside of the cake ring.

3. Put the cake scraps inside the ring and use the back of your hand to tamp the scraps together into a flat even layer.

4. Dunk a pastry brush in the pistachio oil and give the layer of cake a good, healthy bath of half of the oil.

5. Use the back of a spoon to spread half of the lemon curd in an even layer over the cake.

6. Sprinkle one-third of the milk crumbs evenly over the lemon curd. Use the back of your hand to anchor them in place.

7. Use the back of a spoon to spread one-third of the pistachio frosting as evenly as possible over the crumbs.

recipe continues

layer 2, the middle

8. With your index finger, gently tuck the second strip of acetate between the cake ring and the top ¼ inch of the first strip of acetate, so that you have a clear ring of acetate 5 to 6 inches tall—high enough to support the height of the finished cake. Set a cake round on top of the frosting, and repeat the process for layer 1 (if 1 of your 2 cake rounds is jankier than the other, use it here in the middle and save the prettier one for the top).

layer 3, the top

9. Nestle the remaining cake round into the frosting. Cover the top of the cake with the remaining frosting. Give it volume and swirls, or do as we do and opt for a perfectly flat top. Garnish the frosting with the remaining milk crumbs.

10. Transfer the sheet pan to the freezer and freeze for a minimum of 12 hours to set the cake and filling. The cake will keep in the freezer for up to 2 weeks.

11. At least 3 hours before you are ready to serve the cake, pull the sheet pan out of the freezer and, using your fingers and thumbs, pop the cake out of the cake ring. Gently peel off the acetate, and transfer the cake to a platter or cake stand. Let it defrost in the fridge for a minimum of 3 hours (wrapped well in plastic, the cake can be refrigerated for up to 5 days).

12. Slice the cake into wedges and serve.

pistachio cake

MAKES 1 QUARTER SHEET PAN CAKE

In a pinch, substitute 35 g (2 tablespoons) corn syrup for the glucose.

If you substitute 150 g (1½ cups) blanched almond flour for the flour, this becomes a gluten-free cake! Almond flour can be found online, at Whole Foods, or you can make it yourself: In a food processor, grind blanched almonds down to a powder!

Grapeseed oil can be subbed for the pistachio oil, but part of the toasted-pistachio depth of flavor will be lost.

190 g	pistachio paste (see page 20)	⅔ cup
75 g	glucose	3 tablespoons
6	egg whites	
280 g	confectioners' sugar	1¾ cups
110 g	blanched almond flour	1¼ cups
75 g	pistachio oil	½ cup
55 g	heavy cream	¼ cup
160 g	flour	1 cup
6 g	baking powder	1½ teaspoons
6 g	kosher salt	1½ teaspoons
	Pam or other nonstick cooking spray (optional)	

1. Heat the oven to 350°F.

2. Combine the pistachio paste and glucose in the bowl of a stand mixer fitted with the paddle attachment and beat on medium-low for 2 to 3 minutes, until the mixture turns into a sticky green paste. Scrape down the sides of the bowl with a spatula.

3. On low speed, add the egg whites one at a time, being careful not to add the next egg white until the previous one is completely incorporated. Stop the mixer and scrape down the sides of the bowl with a spatula after every 2 to 3 egg whites. Once all of the egg whites have been incorporated, you will have a snotty green soup in your mixing bowl. Right on.

4. Add the confectioners' sugar and almond flour and, on low speed, paddle them in for 2 to 3 minutes, until the mixture thickens. Stop the mixer and scrape down the sides of the bowl.

5. Stream in the pistachio oil and heavy cream and paddle on low speed for 1 minute. Stop the mixer and scrape down the sides of the bowl.

6. Add the flour, baking powder, and salt and paddle on low for 2 to 3 minutes, until the batter is super-smooth and slightly more viscous than your average American box cake batter.

7. Pam-spray a quarter sheet pan and line it with parchment, or just line the pan with a Silpat. Using a spatula, spread the cake batter in an even layer in the pan. Bake for 20 to 22 minutes. The cake will rise and puff, doubling in size. (This cake will become spongy, unlike any of our butter-based cakes, as it has so many egg whites in it.) At 20 minutes, gently poke the edge of the cake with your finger: the cake should bounce back (like said sponge), and it should be slightly golden brown on the sides and pulling away from the sides of the pan ever so slightly. Leave the cake in the oven for an extra 1 to 2 minutes if it doesn't pass these tests.

8. Take the cake out of the oven and cool on a wire rack or, in a pinch, in the fridge or freezer (don't worry, it's not cheating). The cooled cake can be stored in the fridge, wrapped in plastic wrap, for up to 5 days.

lemon curd

MAKES ABOUT 460 G (2 CUPS)

3	lemons	
100 g	sugar	½ cup
4	eggs	
1	gelatin sheet	
115 g	butter, very cold	8 tablespoons (1 stick)
2 g	kosher salt	½ teaspoon

Powdered gelatin can be substituted for the sheet gelatin: use ½ teaspoon.

1. Using a Microplane or the finest-toothed side of a box grater, zest the lemons. Do your best to grate only as far down as the yellow part of the skin; the white pith has less lemon flavor and can be bitter. Squeeze 80 g (⅓ cup) juice from the lemons.

2. Put the sugar, lemon zest, and lemon juice in a blender and blend until the sugar granules have dissolved. Add the eggs and blend on low until you have a bright-yellow mixture. Transfer the contents of the blender to a medium pot or saucepan. Clean the blender canister.

3. Bloom the gelatin (see page 29).

4. Heat the lemon mixture over low heat, whisking regularly. As it heats up, it will begin to thicken; keep a close eye on it. Once it boils, remove it from the stove and transfer it to the blender. Add the bloomed gelatin, butter, and salt and blend until the mixture is thick, shiny, and super-smooth.

5. Pour the mixture through a fine-mesh sieve into a heatproof container, and put in the fridge until the lemon curd has cooled completely, at least 30 minutes. The curd can be refrigerated for up to 1 week; do not freeze.

Elsewhere in this book: Lemon curd is used in the Lemon Mascarpone (page 203) for the Thai Tea Parfait dessert (page 201) and in the Lemon Meringue–Pistachio Pie (page 198).

pistachio frosting

MAKES ABOUT 350 G (1¾ CUPS)

115 g	butter, at room temperature	8 tablespoons (1 stick)	
40 g	confectioners' sugar	¼ cup	
230 g	pistachio paste (see page 20)	¾ cup	
2 g	kosher salt	½ teaspoon	

1. Combine the butter and confectioners' sugar in the bowl of a stand mixer fitted with the paddle attachment and cream together on medium-high for 2 to 3 minutes, until fluffy and pale yellow.

2. Add the pistachio paste and salt and mix on low speed for half a minute, then kick up the speed to medium-high and let her rip for 2 minutes. Scrape down the sides of the bowl with a spatula. If the mixture is not all the same pale green color, give it another minute on high speed, and scrape down again.

3. Use the frosting immediately, or store it in an airtight container in the fridge for up to 1 week.

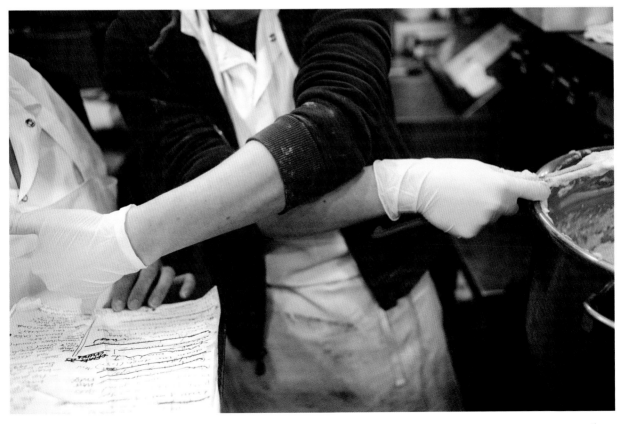

chocolate-chocolate cookies

MAKES 10 TO 15 COOKIES

An ode to my favorite baked good of all time, the fudgy brownie, this cookie has a healthy salt content and, to me, is perfection. I freeze a few of these in the dense heat of a New York summer for my lunch or afternoon snack.

In a pinch, substitute 35 g (2 tablespoons) corn syrup for the glucose.

225 g	butter, at room temperature	16 tablespoons (2 sticks)
300 g	sugar	1½ cups
100 g	glucose	¼ cup
1	egg	
1 g	vanilla extract	¼ teaspoon
60 g	55% chocolate, melted	2 ounces
200 g	flour	1¼ cups
100 g	cocoa powder, preferably Valrhona	¾ cup
3 g	baking powder	¾ teaspoon
1.5 g	baking soda	¼ teaspoon
7 g	kosher salt	1¾ teaspoons
½ recipe	Chocolate Crumb (page 77)	

1. Combine the butter, sugar, and glucose in the bowl of a stand mixer fitted with the paddle attachment and cream together on medium-high for 2 to 3 minutes. Scrape down the sides of the bowl, add the egg, vanilla, and melted chocolate, and beat for 7 to 8 minutes. (See page 27 for notes on this process.)

2. Reduce the mixer speed to low and add the flour, cocoa powder, baking powder, baking soda, and salt. Mix just until the dough comes together, no longer than 1 minute. (Do not walk away from the machine during this step, or you will risk overmixing the dough.) Scrape down the sides of the bowl with a spatula.

3. Still on low speed, add the chocolate crumbs and mix just until incorporated, about 30 seconds.

4. Using a 2¾-ounce ice cream scoop (or a ⅓-cup measure), portion out the dough onto a parchment-lined sheet pan. Pat the tops of the cookie dough domes flat. Wrap the sheet pan tightly in plastic wrap and refrigerate for at least 1 hour, or up to 1 week. Do *not* bake your cookies from room temperature—they will not bake properly.

5. Heat the oven to 375°F.

6. Arrange the chilled dough a minimum of 4 inches apart on parchment- or Silpat-lined sheet pans. Bake for 18 minutes. The cookies will puff, crackle, and spread. It's tough (kind of impossible) to gauge if a cookie that is this dark with chocolate is done. If after 18 minutes, the cookies still seem doughy in the center, give them another 1 minute in the oven, but not more.

7. Cool the cookies completely on the sheet pans before transferring to a plate or an airtight container for storage. At room temp, the cookies will keep fresh for 5 days; in the freezer, they will keep for 1 month.

banana cream pie

MAKES 1 (10-INCH) PIE; SERVES 8 TO 10

1 recipe	Banana Cream (recipe follows)
1 recipe	Chocolate Crust (recipe follows)
1	banana, just ripe, sliced

Pour half of the banana cream into the pie shell. Cover it with a layer of sliced bananas, then cover the bananas with the remaining banana cream. The pie should be stored in the fridge and eaten within a day of when you make it.

banana cream

MAKES ABOUT 775 G (3 CUPS)

You *have* to plan ahead for this one. Buy bananas that are ripe and then let them get nearly black/brown before accepting them as the *rrrrrripe* bananas needed for this recipe. Another great option: at the bakery, we peel just ripe bananas, freeze them, and let them finish developing flavor in the freezer for 2 days or up to 2 weeks. Said *rrrrrripe* bananas are the difference between having your banana pie tasting like banana Laffy Taffy and the most delicious, deep banana cream pie ever.

225 g	*rrrrrripe* bananas	about 2
75 g	heavy cream	⅓ cup
55 g	milk	¼ cup
100 g	sugar	½ cup
25 g	cornstarch	2 tablespoons
2 g	kosher salt	½ teaspoon
3	egg yolks	
2	gelatin sheets	
40 g	butter	3 tablespoons
25 drops	yellow food coloring	½ teaspoon
160 g	heavy cream	¾ cup
160 g	confectioners' sugar	1 cup

Powdered gelatin can be substituted for the sheet gelatin: use 1 teaspoon.

1. Combine the bananas, cream, and milk in a blender and puree until totally smooth.

2. Add the sugar, cornstarch, salt, and yolks and continue to blend until homogenous. Pour the mixture into a medium saucepan. Clean the blender canister.

3. Bloom the gelatin (see page 29).

4. Whisk the contents of the pan and heat over medium-low heat. As the banana mixture heats up, it will thicken. Bring to a boil and then continue to whisk vigorously for 2 minutes to fully cook out the starch. The mixture will resemble thick glue, bordering on cement, with a color to match.

5. Dump the contents of the pan into the blender. Add the bloomed gelatin and the butter and blend until the mixture is smooth and even. Color the

Elsewhere in this book: Banana cream is used in the Banana Layer Cake (page 193). The cream also tastes great when layered with Cereal Milk Panna Cotta (page 37).

recipe continues

mixture with yellow food coloring until it is a bright cartoon-banana yellow. (It's a *ton* of coloring, I know, but banana creams don't get that brilliant yellow color on their own. Womp.)

6. Transfer the banana mixture to a heatsafe container, and put in the fridge for 30 to 60 minutes—as long as it takes to cool completely.

7. Using a whisk or a mixer with the whisk attachment, whip the cream and confectioners' sugar to medium-soft peaks. (When you pull the whisk away from the whipped cream, the mounds of cream hold their shape softly.) Add the cold banana mixture to the whipped cream and slowly whisk until evenly colored and homogenous. Stored in an airtight container, banana cream keeps fresh for up to 5 days in the fridge.

chocolate crust

MAKES 1 (10-INCH) PIE CRUST

Making this pie shell is the perfect opportunity to use some of those disposable kitchen gloves we recommend (see page 23) to keep your hands from looking like a mechanic's that just changed someone's oil.

¾ recipe	Chocolate Crumb (page 77)	260 g (1¾ cups)
8 g	sugar	2 teaspoons
0.5 g	kosher salt	⅛ teaspoon
14 g	butter, melted, or as needed	1 tablespoon

1. Pulse the chocolate crumbs in a food processor until they are sandy and no sizeable clusters remain.

2. Transfer the sand to a bowl and, with your hands, toss with the sugar and salt. Add the melted butter and knead it into the sand until it is moist enough to knead into a ball. If it is not moist enough to do so, melt an additional 14 g (1 tablespoon) butter and knead it in.

3. Transfer the mixture to a 10-inch pie tin. With your fingers and the palms of your hands, press the chocolate crust firmly into the tin, making sure the bottom and sides of the pie tin are evenly covered. Wrapped in plastic wrap, the crust can be stored at room temp for up to 5 days or in the fridge for 2 weeks.

Elsewhere in this book: The chocolate crust is used in Candy Bar Pie (page 174).

chocolate chip layer cake

MAKES 1 (6-INCH) LAYER CAKE, 5 TO 6 INCHES TALL; SERVES 6 TO 8

Passion fruit, chocolate, and coffee is one of my favorite flavor trios. Though the combo sounds a little out there, it's actually beloved in lots of pastry kitchens. I wanted a way to feature it in a mainstream dessert. Turns out a deep vanilla chocolate chip layer cake is the perfect fit.

1 recipe	Chocolate Chip Cake (recipe follows)	
60 g	passion fruit puree	⅓ cup
1 recipe	Passion Fruit Curd (recipe follows)	
½ recipe	Chocolate Crumb (page 77)	
1 recipe	Coffee Frosting (recipe follows)	
40 g	mini chocolate chips	¼ cup

special equipment

1 (6-inch) cake ring

2 strips acetate, each 3 inches wide and 20 inches long

1. Put a piece of parchment or a Silpat on the counter. Invert the cake onto it and peel off the parchment or Silpat from the bottom of the cake. Use the cake ring to stamp out 2 circles from the cake. These are your top 2 cake layers. The remaining cake "scrap" will come together to make the bottom layer of the cake.

layer 1, the bottom
2. Clean the cake ring and place it in the center of a sheet pan lined with clean parchment or a Silpat. Use 1 strip of acetate to line the inside of the cake ring.

3. Put the cake scraps inside the ring and use the back of your hand to tamp the scraps together into a flat even layer.

4. Dunk a pastry brush in the passion fruit puree and give the layer of cake a good, healthy bath of half of the puree.

5. Use the back of a spoon to spread half of the passion fruit curd in an even layer over the cake.

6. Sprinkle half of the chocolate crumbs evenly over the passion fruit curd. Use the back of your hand to anchor them in place.

recipe continues

7. Use the back of a spoon to spread one-third of the coffee frosting as evenly as possible over the chocolate crumbs.

layer 2, the middle

8. With your index finger, gently tuck the second strip of acetate between the cake ring and the top ¼ inch of the first strip of acetate, so that you have a clear ring of acetate 5 to 6 inches tall—high enough to support the height of the finished cake. Set a cake round on top of the frosting, and repeat the process for layer 1 (if 1 of your 2 cake rounds is jankier than the other, use it here in the middle and save the prettier one for the top).

layer 3, the top

9. Nestle the remaining cake round into the frosting. Cover the top of the cake with the remaining frosting. Give it volume and swirls, or do as we do and opt for a perfectly flat top. Garnish the frosting with the mini chocolate chips.

10. Transfer the sheet pan to the freezer and freeze for a minimum of 12 hours to set the cake and filling. The cake will keep in the freezer for up to 2 weeks.

11. At least 3 hours before you are ready to serve the cake, pull the sheet pan out of the freezer and, using your fingers and thumbs, pop the cake out of the cake ring. Gently peel off the acetate, and transfer the cake to a platter or cake stand. Let it defrost in the fridge for a minimum of 3 hours (wrapped well in plastic, it can be refrigerated for up to 5 days).

12. Slice the cake into wedges and serve.

chocolate chip cake

MAKES 1 QUARTER SHEET PAN CAKE

Happy birthday, Dave Chang! That's what the kitchen screamed when we first made this cake. Marian was in charge of making boss man a birthday cake. She told me she channeled her innermost version of me, sprinkled chocolate chips into a vanilla cake batter we were going to use as a coconut cake, and layered it with liquid cheesecake and anything else she could find in the fridge; in other words, she followed to a tee our standard operating procedure for any birthday cake in our kitchen. Now even the Momofuku savory cooks know this cake by heart. It is a snack attack waiting to happen, so you may want to consider making a double batch of batter and baking the cake in a half sheet pan.

recipe continues

115 g	butter, at room temperature	8 tablespoons (1 stick)
250 g	granulated sugar	1¼ cups
60 g	light brown sugar	¼ cup tightly packed
3	eggs	
110 g	buttermilk	½ cup
75 g	grapeseed oil	½ cup
12 g	vanilla extract	1 tablespoon
185 g	cake flour	1½ cups
4 g	baking powder	1 teaspoon
4 g	kosher salt	1 teaspoon
	Pam or other nonstick cooking spray (optional)	
150 g	mini chocolate chips	¾ cup

There is a *ton* of liquid and fat in this amazing cake! If you do not do your due diligence to make sure that the batter is homogenous at each step (no streaks, discolorations, or other signs of separation/unincorporation), you'll be sorry when your cake bakes out of its pan and all over the bottom of your oven.

1. Heat the oven to 350°F.

2. Combine the butter and sugars in the bowl of a stand mixer fitted with the paddle attachment and cream together on medium-high for 2 to 3 minutes. Scrape down the sides of the bowl, add the eggs, and mix on medium-high again for 2 to 3 minutes. Scrape down the sides of the bowl once more.

3. On low speed, stream in the buttermilk, oil, and vanilla. Increase the mixer speed to medium-high and paddle for 4 to 6 minutes, until the mixture is practically white, twice the size of your original fluffy butter-and-sugar mixture, and completely homogenous. Don't rush the process. You're basically forcing too much liquid into an already fatty mixture that doesn't want to make room for the liquid. Stop the mixer and scrape down the sides of the bowl.

4. On very low speed, add the cake flour, baking powder, and salt. Mix for 45 to 60 seconds, just until your batter comes together and any remnants of dry ingredients have been incorporated. Scrape down the sides of the bowl. If you see any lumps of cake flour in there while you're scraping, mix for another 45 seconds.

5. Pam-spray a quarter sheet pan and line it with parchment, or just line the pan with a Silpat. Using a spatula, spread the cake batter in an even layer in the pan. Give the bottom of your sheet pan a tap on the countertop to even out the layer. Sprinkle the chocolate chips evenly over the cake batter.

6. Bake the cake for 30 to 35 minutes. The cake will rise and puff, doubling in size, but will remain slightly buttery and dense. At 30 minutes, gently poke the edge of the cake with your finger: the cake should bounce back slightly and the center should no longer be jiggly. Leave the cake in the oven for an extra 3 to 5 minutes if it doesn't pass these tests.

7. Take the cake out of the oven and cool on a wire rack or, in a pinch, in the fridge or freezer (don't worry, it's not cheating). The cooled cake can be stored in the fridge, wrapped in plastic wrap, for up to 5 days.

passion fruit curd

MAKES ABOUT 360 G (1½ CUPS)

This recipe is similar to the grapefruit pie's Grapefruit Passion Curd (page 68), but with slightly different ingredient proportions. It also makes a larger batch so there's enough to fill the chocolate chip cake.

100 g	passion fruit puree	½ cup
65 g	sugar	⅓ cup
2	eggs	
1	gelatin sheet	
170 g	butter, very cold	12 tablespoons (1½ sticks)
2 g	kosher salt	½ teaspoon

Powdered gelatin can be substituted for the gelatin sheets: use ½ teaspoon.

1. Put the passion fruit puree and sugar in a blender and blend until the sugar granules have dissolved. Add the eggs and blend on low until you have a bright-orange-yellow mixture. Transfer the contents of the blender to a medium pot or saucepan. Clean the blender canister.

2. Bloom the gelatin (see page 29).

3. Heat the passion fruit mixture over low heat, whisking regularly. As it heats up, it will begin to thicken; keep a close eye on it. Once it boils, remove it from the stove and transfer it to the blender. Add the bloomed gelatin, butter, and salt and blend until the mixture is thick, shiny, and super-smooth.

4. Transfer the mixture to a heatproof container, and put in the fridge until the curd has cooled completely, at least 30 minutes. The curd can be refrigerated for up to 1 week; do not freeze.

coffee frosting

MAKES ABOUT 200 G (1 CUP)

Do not make this recipe until you are ready to assemble the chocolate chip cake. Once it is cold, coffee frosting is hell to bring back up to room temp. It will separate on you, and you will spend the same amount of time trying to force the coffee milk back into the butter mixture.

We use Nescafé instant coffee for this delicious frosting. The entire country of Greece makes an amazing frappe that puts Starbucks' frappuccino to shame, and Nescafé is the secret ingredient.

115 g	butter, at room temperature	8 tablespoons (1 stick)
40 g	confectioners' sugar	¼ cup
55 g	milk	¼ cup
1.5 g	instant coffee powder	¾ teaspoon
1 g	kosher salt	¼ teaspoon

1. Combine the butter and confectioners' sugar in the bowl of a stand mixer fitted with the paddle attachment and cream together on medium-high for 2 to 3 minutes, until fluffy and pale yellow.

2. Meanwhile, make a quick coffee milk: whisk together the milk, instant coffee, and salt in a small bowl.

3. Scrape down the sides of the bowl with a spatula. On low speed, gradually stream in the coffee milk. You are essentially forcing liquid into fat, so be patient. The butter mixture will clump up and separate upon contact with the coffee milk. Do not stream more coffee milk into the butter mixture until the previous addition is fully incorporated; keep the mixer on and remain patient. The result will be a wildly fluffy coffee frosting, pale brown and super-shiny. Use immediately.

confetti cookies

MAKES 15 TO 20 COOKIES

When we were in the Spanish Harlem rental kitchen for the summer of 2010, our cornflake-chocolate-chip-marshmallow cookie just wouldn't bake up right in the busted convection ovens we were forced to use. So we stopped our crying, stopped making the cookie for a while, and took the opportunity to bring a new cookie into creation. The confetti cookie combines the technique of a snickerdoodle (cream of tartar makes all the difference in telling an average cookie apart from a snickerdoodle-inspired one) with the flavors of funfetti cake mix.

In a pinch, substitute 25 g (1 tablespoon) corn syrup for the glucose.

225 g	butter, at room temperature	16 tablespoons (2 sticks)
300 g	sugar	1½ cups
50 g	glucose	2 tablespoons
2	eggs	
8 g	*clear* vanilla extract (see page 21)	2 teaspoons
400 g	flour	2½ cups
50 g	milk powder	⅔ cup
9 g	cream of tartar	2 teaspoons
6 g	baking soda	1 teaspoon
5 g	kosher salt	1¼ teaspoons
40 g	rainbow sprinkles	¼ cup
½ recipe	Birthday Cake Crumb (page 78)	

1. Combine the butter, sugar, and glucose in the bowl of a stand mixer fitted with the paddle attachment and cream together on medium-high for 2 to 3 minutes. Scrape down the sides of the bowl, add the eggs and vanilla, and beat for 7 to 8 minutes. (See page 27 for notes on this process.)

2. Reduce the mixer speed to low and add the flour, milk powder, cream of tartar, baking soda, salt, and rainbow sprinkles. Mix just until the dough comes together, no longer than 1 minute. (Do not walk away from the machine during this step, or you will risk overmixing the dough.) Scrape down the sides of the bowl with a spatula.

3. Still on low speed, add the birthday cake crumbs and mix in for 30 seconds—just until they are incorporated.

4. Using a 2¾-ounce ice cream scoop (or a ⅓-cup measure), portion out the dough onto a parchment-lined sheet pan. Pat the tops of the cookie dough domes flat. Wrap the sheet pan tightly in plastic wrap and refrigerate for at least 1 hour, or up to 1 week. Do *not* bake your cookies from room temperature—they will not bake properly.

5. Heat the oven to 350°F.

6. Arrange the chilled dough a minimum of 4 inches apart on parchment- or Silpat-lined sheet pans. Bake for 18 minutes. The cookies will puff, crackle, and spread. After 18 minutes, they should be very lightly browned on the edges (golden brown on the bottom). The centers will show just the beginning signs of color. Leave the cookies in the oven for an additional minute or so if the colors don't match and the cookies still seem pale and doughy on the surface.

7. Cool the cookies completely on the sheet pans before transferring to a plate or an airtight container for storage. At room temp, the cookies will keep fresh for 5 days; in the freezer, they will keep for 1 month.

birthday layer cake

MAKES 1 (6-INCH) LAYER CAKE, 5 TO 6 INCHES TALL; SERVES 6 TO 8

Once we got birthday cake crumbs down, we moved on to our larger quest of making a funfetti cake, canned frosting and all, from scratch. Turns out that looking on the side of the cake mix box at the monster ingredient list was really helpful in getting the "secret" stuff we couldn't figure out by taste.

1 recipe	Birthday Cake (recipe follows)
1 recipe	Birthday Cake Soak (recipe follows)
1 recipe	Birthday Cake Frosting (recipe follows)
1 recipe	Birthday Cake Crumb (page 78)

special equipment

1 (6-inch) cake ring

2 strips acetate, each 3 inches wide and 20 inches long

1. Put a piece of parchment or a Silpat on the counter. Invert the cake onto it and peel off the parchment or Silpat from the bottom of the cake. Use the cake ring to stamp out 2 circles from the cake. These are your top 2 cake layers. The remaining cake "scrap" will come together to make the bottom layer of the cake.

layer 1, the bottom

2. Clean the cake ring and place it in the center of a sheet pan lined with clean parchment or a Silpat. Use 1 strip of acetate to line the inside of the cake ring.

3. Put the cake scraps in the ring and use the back of your hand to tamp the scraps together into a flat even layer.

4. Dunk a pastry brush in the birthday cake soak and give the layer of cake a good, healthy bath of half of the soak.

5. Use the back of a spoon to spread one-fifth of the frosting in an even layer over the cake.

6. Sprinkle one-third of the birthday crumbs evenly over the top of the frosting. Use the back of your hand to anchor them in place.

7. Use the back of a spoon to spread a second fifth of the frosting as evenly as possible over the crumbs.

layer 2, the middle

8. With your index finger, gently tuck the second strip of acetate between the cake ring and the top ¼ inch of the first strip of acetate, so that you have a clear ring of acetate 5 to 6 inches tall—high enough to support the height of the finished cake. Set a cake round on top of the frosting, and repeat the process for layer 1 (if 1 of your 2 cake rounds is jankier than the other, use it here in the middle and save the prettier one for the top).

layer 3, the top

9. Nestle the remaining cake round into the frosting. Cover the top of the cake with the last fifth of the frosting. Give it volume and swirls, or do as we do and opt for a perfectly flat top. Garnish the frosting with the remaining birthday crumbs.

10. Transfer the sheet pan to the freezer and freeze for a minimum of 12 hours to set the cake and filling. The cake will keep in the freezer for up to 2 weeks.

11. At least 3 hours before you are ready to serve the cake, pull the sheet pan out of the freezer and, using your fingers and thumbs, pop the cake out of the cake ring. Gently peel off the acetate and transfer the cake to a platter or cake stand. Let it defrost in the fridge for a minimum of 3 hours (wrapped well in plastic, it can be refrigerated for up to 5 days).

12. Slice the cake into wedges and serve.

birthday cake

MAKES 1 QUARTER SHEET PAN CAKE

55 g	butter, at room temperature	4 tablespoons (½ stick)
60 g	vegetable shortening	⅓ cup
250 g	granulated sugar	1¼ cups
50 g	light brown sugar	3 tablespoons tightly packed
3	eggs	
110 g	buttermilk	½ cup
65 g	grapeseed oil	⅓ cup
8 g	*clear* vanilla extract (see page 21)	2 teaspoons
245 g	cake flour	2 cups
6 g	baking powder	1½ teaspoons
3 g	kosher salt	¾ teaspoon
50 g	rainbow sprinkles	¼ cup
	Pam or other nonstick cooking spray (optional)	
25 g	rainbow sprinkles	2 tablespoons

1. Heat the oven to 350°F.

2. Combine the butter, shortening, and sugars in the bowl of a stand mixer fitted with the paddle attachment and cream together on medium-high for 2 to 3 minutes. Scrape down the sides of the bowl, add the eggs, and mix on medium-high for 2 to 3 minutes. Scrape down the sides of the bowl once more.

3. On low speed, stream in the buttermilk, oil, and vanilla. Increase the mixer speed to medium-high and paddle for 4 to 6 minutes, until the mixture is practically white, twice the size of your original fluffy butter-and-sugar mixture, and completely homogenous. Don't rush the process. You're basically forcing too much liquid into an already fatty mixture that doesn't want to make room for the liquid. There should be no streaks of fat or liquid. Stop the mixer and scrape down the sides of the bowl.

4. On very low speed, add the cake flour, baking powder, salt, and the 50 g (¼ cup) rainbow sprinkles. Mix for 45 to 60 seconds, just until your batter comes together. Scrape down the sides of the bowl.

recipe continues

5. Pam-spray a quarter sheet pan and line it with parchment, or just line the pan with a Silpat. Using a spatula, spread the cake batter in an even layer in the pan. Sprinkle the remaining 25 g (2 tablespoons) rainbow sprinkles evenly on top of the batter.

6. Bake the cake for 30 to 35 minutes. The cake will rise and puff, doubling in size, but will remain slightly buttery and dense. At 30 minutes, gently poke the edge of the cake with your finger: the cake should bounce back slightly and the center should no longer be jiggly. Leave the cake in the oven for an extra 3 to 5 minutes if it doesn't pass these tests.

7. Take the cake out of the oven and cool on a wire rack or, in a pinch, in the fridge or freezer (don't worry, it's not cheating). The cooled cake can be stored in the fridge, wrapped in plastic wrap, for up to 5 days.

birthday cake soak

MAKES ABOUT 60 G (¼ CUP)

55 g	milk	¼ cup
4 g	*clear* vanilla extract (see page 21)	1 teaspoon

Whisk together the milk and vanilla in a small bowl.

birthday cake frosting

MAKES ABOUT 430 G (2 CUPS)

115 g	butter, at room temperature	8 tablespoons (1 stick)
50 g	vegetable shortening	¼ cup
55 g	cream cheese	2 ounces
25 g	glucose	1 tablespoon
18 g	corn syrup	1 tablespoon
12 g	*clear* vanilla extract (see page 21)	1 tablespoon
200 g	confectioners' sugar	1¼ cups
2 g	kosher salt	½ teaspoon
0.25 g	baking powder	pinch
0.25 g	citric acid (see page 16)	pinch

In a pinch, substitute 12 g (2 teaspoons) corn syrup for the glucose.

1. Combine the butter, shortening, and cream cheese in the bowl of a stand mixer fitted with the paddle attachment and cream together on medium-high for 2 to 3 minutes, until the mixture is smooth and fluffy. Scrape down the sides of the bowl.

2. With the mixer on its lowest speed, stream in the glucose, corn syrup, and vanilla. Crank the mixer up to medium-high and beat for 2 to 3 minutes, until the mixture is silky smooth and a glossy white. Scrape down the sides of the bowl.

3. Add the confectioners' sugar, salt, baking powder, and citric acid and mix on low speed just to incorporate them into the batter. Crank the speed back up to medium-high and beat for 2 to 3 minutes, until you have a brilliant stark white, beautifully smooth frosting. It should look just like it came out of a plastic tub at the grocery store! Use the frosting immediately, or store it in an airtight container in the fridge for up to 1 week.

graham

crust

As a kid back in Virginia, I became obsessed with Jell-O cheesecake mix. There were two packets in the box: one packet held the graham crumbs that you made into a crust following the recipe on the side of the box. I used to throw that packet out and go straight for the jugular: the cheesecake filling.

See, the graham crumb packet called for milk, some margarine, a bit of salt, and a pinch of sugar. Made with the skim milk found in my house and "I Can't Believe It's Not Butter!" or another lame butter alternative, it always tasted like a dull, soggy mess. So I didn't waste my time. I was a young cook, with no real knowledge of the subtleties of ingredients and their flavors. I just knew what tasted good and right, and, conversely, what was gross. But I didn't know how to make something taste better: how to sharpen flavors or refine recipes within the realm of sweet, salty, or buttery. It wasn't until years later that I honed these skills.

Salted caramel stole my heart in the early nineties, when it really made its way into mainstream media with its buttery-sweet start and buttery-salty finish. A dream come true, and a case study for me in terms of the power of ratios when dealing with my favorite ingredients. That balance is what I identify with first and foremost, even today.

During my twenties, I spent a lot of time learning about food, reading cookbooks, experimenting with recipes, and gaining a better overall understanding of certain ingredients, such as the difference between graham crusts made with milk or heavy cream or melted butter. It turns out there was more than one way to make a graham crust, and it didn't require a Jell-O cheesecake mix.

Ten years later, I had a kitchen of my own, and I decided it was high time I came up with my own graham crust recipe. The perfect ratios of salt, sugar, and melted butter were the foundation, I knew. But I wanted my crust to stick out even more. I had discovered the power of milk powder earlier while experimenting with milk crumbs in the basement at Ssäm Bar. And at that point, I was putting milk powder in every baked good, just to see what might happen. In the graham crust recipe, it added an amazing depth of flavor and a chewiness to the final product that I just loved.

To this day, the graham crust passes my snack test. Whenever anyone has a tub of it out on a prep table, I swoop in, scoop some into my hand, and snack away, happy as ever.

graham crust

MAKES ABOUT 340 G (2 CUPS)

190 g	graham cracker crumbs	1½ cups
20 g	milk powder	¼ cup
25 g	sugar	2 tablespoons
3 g	kosher salt	¾ teaspoon
55 g	butter, melted, or as needed	4 tablespoons (½ stick)
55 g	heavy cream	¼ cup

1. Toss the graham crumbs, milk powder, sugar, and salt with your hands in a medium bowl to evenly distribute your dry ingredients.

2. Whisk the butter and heavy cream together. Add to the dry ingredients and toss again to evenly distribute. The butter will act as a glue, adhering to the dry ingredients and turning the mixture into a bunch of small clusters. The mixture should hold its shape if squeezed tightly in the palm of your hand. If it is not moist enough to do so, melt an additional 14 to 25 g (1 to 1½ tablespoons) butter and mix it in.

3. Eat immediately, or deploy as directed in a recipe. The crust is easiest to mold just after mixing. Stored in an airtight container, graham crust will keep fresh for 1 week at room temperature or for 1 month in the fridge or freezer.

graham ice cream

MAKES ABOUT 550 G (1 PINT)

¼ recipe	Graham Crust (page 112)	85 g (½ cup)
220 g	milk	1 cup
2	gelatin sheets	
160 g	heavy cream	¾ cup
100 g	glucose	¼ cup
65 g	sugar	⅓ cup
40 g	milk powder	½ cup
1 g	kosher salt	¼ teaspoon

Powdered gelatin can be substituted for the sheet gelatin: use 1 teaspoon. In a pinch, substitute 35 g (2 tablespoons) corn syrup for the glucose.

Toasting the graham crust before steeping deepens the flavor of the milk.

Instead of a whisk, use a hand blender to mix the ice cream base.

1. Heat the oven to 250°F.

2. Dump the graham crust onto a parchment- or Silpat-lined sheet pan and spread it out evenly. Bake for 15 minutes to toast it lightly and deepen its flavor. Cool completely.

3. Transfer the cooled graham crust to a pitcher. Pour in the milk and stir. Let steep for 20 minutes at room temperature.

4. Strain the mixture through a fine-mesh sieve into a medium bowl. The milk will drain off quickly at first, then become thicker and starchy toward the end of the straining process. Using the back of a ladle (or your hand) wring the milk out of the toasted graham crust, but do not force the mushy graham crust through the sieve. Discard said mush.

5. Bloom the gelatin (see page 29).

6. Warm a little bit of the graham milk and whisk in the gelatin to dissolve. Whisk in the remaining graham milk, the heavy cream, glucose, sugar, milk powder, and salt until everything is fully dissolved and incorporated.

7. Pour the mixture through a fine-mesh sieve into your ice cream machine and freeze according to the manufacturer's instructions. The ice cream is best spun just before serving or using, but it will keep in an airtight container in the freezer for up to 2 weeks.

compost cookies

MAKES 15 TO 20 COOKIES

When I was a baker at a conference center on Star Island, twelve miles off the coast of New Hampshire, I learned to make this kind of cookie from one of the best bakers I know, Mandy Lamb. She would put different ingredients in the cookie each day or each week and have people try and guess what the random secret ingredients were.

Because we were on an island in New England, when storms blew in, we were trapped. No one traveled to the island, and, more important, no boats with food on them came our way, either. We had to get creative and use what we had on hand. We might not have had enough chocolate chips to make chocolate chip cookies, but if we threw in other mix-ins as well, the seven hundred some guests would never notice the shortage of one ingredient—and the cookies would always feel brand new, because they were different every time. I found after many batches that my favorite compost cookies had my favorite snacks in them: chocolate and butter-scotch chips, potato chips, pretzels, graham crackers, and coffee (grounds).

Compost cookies always turn out great in my mother's kitchen because she infamously has a hodgepodge of mix-ins, none in great enough quantity to make an actual single-flavored cookie on its own. My brother-in-law calls them "garbage cookies"; others call them "kitchen sink cookies." Call them what you want, and make them as we make them at Milk Bar, or add your own favorite snacks to the cookie base in place of ours.

In a pinch, substitute 18 g (1 tablespoon) corn syrup for the glucose.

For the "coffee grounds" in this cookie, we tested the recipe with freshly roasted and ground artisanal coffee from Stumptown as well as with crap-tastic coffee grounds that you can find just about anywhere. We discovered that it doesn't make a difference what kind you use; the cookie is delicious every time. Just make sure you don't use instant coffee; it will dissolve in the baking process and ruin the cookies. And, above all else, never use wet, sogalicious grounds that have already brewed a pot of coffee.

We use Cape Cod potato chips because they aren't paper-thin, and so they do not break down too much in the mixing process.

225 g	butter, at room temperature	16 tablespoons (2 sticks)
200 g	granulated sugar	1 cup
150 g	light brown sugar	⅔ cup tightly packed
50 g	glucose	2 tablespoons
1	egg	
2 g	vanilla extract	½ teaspoon
225 g	flour	1⅓ cups
2 g	baking powder	½ teaspoon
1.5 g	baking soda	¼ teaspoon
4 g	kosher salt	1 teaspoon
150 g	mini chocolate chips	¾ cup
100 g	mini butterscotch chips	½ cup

¼ recipe	Graham Crust (page 112)	85 g (½ cup)	
40 g	old-fashioned rolled oats	⅓ cup	
5 g	ground coffee	2½ teaspoons	

50 g	potato chips	2 cups	
50 g	mini pretzels	1 cup	

1. Combine the butter, sugars, and glucose in the bowl of a stand mixer fitted with the paddle attachment and cream together on medium-high for 2 to 3 minutes. Scrape down the sides of the bowl, add the egg and vanilla, and beat for 7 to 8 minutes. (See page 27 for notes on this process.)

2. Reduce the speed to low and add the flour, baking powder, baking soda, and salt. Mix just until the dough comes together, no longer than 1 minute. (Do not walk away from the machine during this step, or you will risk overmixing the dough.) Scrape down the sides of the bowl with a spatula.

3. Still on low speed, add the chocolate chips, butterscotch chips, graham crust, oats, and coffee and mix just until incorporated, about 30 seconds. Add the potato chips and pretzels and paddle, still on low speed, until just incorporated. Be careful not to overmix or break too many of the pretzels or potato chips. You deserve a pat on the back if one of your cookies bakes off with a whole pretzel standing up in the center.

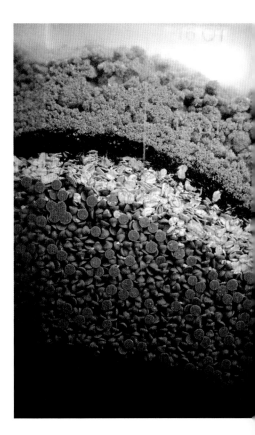

4. Using a 2¾-ounce ice cream scoop (or a ⅓-cup measure), portion out the dough onto a parchment-lined sheet pan. Pat the tops of the cookie dough domes flat. Wrap the sheet pan tightly in plastic wrap and refrigerate for at least 1 hour, or up to 1 week. Do *not* bake your cookies from room temperature—they will not bake properly.

5. Heat the oven to 375°F.

6. Arrange the chilled dough a minimum of 4 inches apart on parchment- or Silpat-lined sheet pans. Bake for 18 minutes. The cookies will puff, crackle, and spread. After 18 minutes, they should be very faintly browned on the edges yet still bright yellow in the center. Give them an extra minute or so if that's not the case.

7. Cool the cookies completely on the sheet pans before transferring to a plate or an airtight container for storage. At room temp, cookies will keep fresh for 5 days; in the freezer, they will keep for 1 month.

carrot layer cake

MAKES 1 (6-INCH) LAYER CAKE, 5 TO 6 INCHES TALL; SERVES 6 TO 8

1 recipe	Carrot Cake (recipe follows)	
55 g	milk	¼ cup
1 recipe	Liquid Cheesecake (page 149)	
½ recipe	Milk Crumb (page 74)	
1 recipe	Graham Frosting (recipe follows)	

special equipment

1 (6-inch) cake ring

2 strips acetate, each 3 inches wide and 20 inches long

1. Put a piece of parchment or a Silpat on the counter. Invert the cake onto it and peel off the parchment or Silpat from the bottom of the cake. Use the cake ring to stamp out 2 circles from the cake. These are your top 2 cake layers. The remaining cake "scrap" will come together to make the bottom layer of the cake.

layer 1, the bottom
2. Clean the cake ring and place it in the center of a sheet pan lined with clean parchment or a Silpat. Use 1 strip of acetate to line the inside of the cake ring.

3. Put the cake scraps inside the ring and use the back of your hand to tamp the scraps together into a flat even layer.

4. Dunk a pastry brush in the milk and give the layer of cake a good, healthy bath of half of the milk.

5. Use the back of a spoon to spread half of the liquid cheesecake in an even layer over the cake.

6. Sprinkle one-third of the milk crumbs evenly over the cheesecake. Use the back of your hand to anchor them in place.

7. Use the back of a spoon to spread one-third of the graham frosting as evenly as possible over the crumbs.

layer 2, the middle
8. With your index finger, gently tuck the second strip of acetate between the cake ring and the top ¼ inch of the first strip of acetate, so that you have a clear ring of acetate 5 to 6 inches tall—high enough to support the height of the finished cake. Set a cake round on top of the frosting, and repeat the process for layer 1 (if 1 of your 2 cake rounds is jankier than the other, use it here in the middle and save the prettier one for the top).

recipe continues

graham crust **117**

layer 3, the top

9. Nestle the remaining cake round into the frosting. Cover the top of the cake with the remaining frosting. Give it volume and swirls, or do as we do and opt for a perfectly flat top. Garnish the frosting with the remaining milk crumbs.

10. Transfer the sheet pan to the freezer and freeze for a minimum of 12 hours to set the cake and filling. The cake will keep in the freezer for up to 2 weeks.

11. At least 3 hours before you are ready to serve the cake, pull the sheet pan out of the freezer and, using your fingers and thumbs, pop the cake out of the cake ring. Gently peel off the acetate and transfer the cake to a platter or cake stand. Let it defrost in the fridge for a minimum of 3 hours (wrapped well in plastic, it can be refrigerated for up to 5 days).

12. Slice the cake into wedges and serve.

carrot cake

MAKES 1 QUARTER SHEET PAN CAKE

My mama is a busy, busy woman. If she were baking this cake, she would probably opt to buy preshredded carrots from the grocery store. She likes baking shortcuts and, in this case, it's quite possible she doesn't know where her box grater is (or if the handle is still attached to it).

I'm not going to lie. I've bought preshredded carrots, and the results weren't one bit terrible. But at the farmers' market, they've got yellow carrots and purple carrots and orange carrots that actually taste like something. And they will make your cake better if you use them.

115 g	butter, at room temperature	8 tablespoons (1 stick)
120 g	light brown sugar	½ cup tightly packed
100 g	granulated sugar	½ cup
2	eggs	
40 g	grapeseed oil	¼ cup
200 g	flour	1¼ cups
4 g	baking powder	1 teaspoon
1.5 g	baking soda	¼ teaspoon
1.5 g	ground cinnamon	¾ teaspoon
5 g	kosher salt	1¼ teaspoons
225 g	shredded peeled carrots (2 to 3 medium-sized carrots)	2½ cups
	Pam or other nonstick cooking spray (optional)	

1. Heat the oven to 350°F.

2. Combine the butter and sugars in the bowl of a stand mixer fitted with the paddle attachment and cream together on medium-high for 2 to 3 minutes. Scrape down the sides of the bowl, add the eggs, and mix on medium-high for 2 to 3 minutes. Scrape down the sides of the bowl once more.

3. On low speed, stream in the oil. Increase the mixer speed to medium-high and paddle for 4 to 6 minutes, until the mixture is practically white, twice the size of your original fluffy butter-and-sugar mixture, and completely

recipe continues

homogenous, with no streaks of fat. Don't rush the process. Stop the mixer and scrape down the sides of the bowl.

4. On very low speed, add the flour, baking powder, baking soda, cinnamon, and salt. Mix for 45 to 60 seconds, just until your batter comes together and any remnants of dry ingredients have been incorporated. Scrape down the sides of the bowl.

5. Detach the paddle and remove the bowl from the mixer. Dump the shredded carrots into the bowl and, with a spatula, fold them into the batter.

6. Pam-spray a quarter sheet pan and line it with parchment, or just line the pan with a Silpat. Using a spatula, spread the cake batter in an even layer in the pan.

7. Bake the cake for 25 to 30 minutes. The cake will rise and puff, doubling in size, but will remain slightly buttery and dense. At 25 minutes, gently poke the edge of the cake with your finger: the cake should bounce back slightly and the center should no longer be jiggly. Leave the cake in the oven for an extra 3 to 5 minutes if it doesn't pass these tests.

8. Take the cake out of the oven and cool on a wire rack or, in a pinch, in the fridge or freezer (don't worry, it's not cheating). The cooled cake can be stored in the fridge, wrapped in plastic wrap, for up to 5 days.

graham frosting

MAKES ABOUT 230 G (1 CUP)

One of our favorite things to do is to make a frosting with an unexpected flavor. For this one, we puree graham crust down to a liquid form and then paddle it into whipping butter with a little seasoning.

½ recipe	Graham Crust (page 112)	
85 g	milk	⅓ cup
2 g	kosher salt	½ teaspoon
85 g	butter, at room temperature	6 tablespoons
15 g	light brown sugar	1 tablespoon tightly packed
10 g	confectioners' sugar	1 tablespoon
0.5 g	ground cinnamon	½ teaspoon
0.5 g	kosher salt	⅛ teaspoon

1. Combine the graham crust, milk, and salt in a blender, turn the speed on to medium-high, and puree until smooth and homogenous. It will take 1 to 3 minutes (depending on the awesomeness of your blender). If the mixture does not catch on your blender blade, turn off the blender, take a small teaspoon, and scrape down the sides of the canister, remembering to scrape under the blade, then try again.

2. Combine the butter, sugars, cinnamon, and salt in the bowl of a stand mixer fitted with the paddle attachment, and cream together on medium-high for 2 to 3 minutes, until fluffy and speckled yellow. Scrape down the sides of the bowl with a spatula.

3. On low speed, paddle in the contents of the blender. After 1 minute, crank the speed up to medium-high and let her rip for another 2 minutes. Scrape down the sides of the bowl with a spatula. If the mixture is not a uniform pale tan, give the bowl another scrape-down and the frosting another minute of high-speed paddling.

4. Use the frosting immediately, or store it in an airtight container in the fridge for up to 1 week.

carrot cake truffles

MAKES TWELVE TO FIFTEEN 30 G (1 OUNCE) BALLS

Our most successful new offering in 2010 was our cake truffles, spawned entirely from leftovers. We had once served slices of cake to order, but after hemming and hawing with our endearing staff of counter employees over the correct way to slice and serve a multilayered cake, we decided to get smart. Helen and Leslie were the catalyst behind convincing me to make cake truffles with all of our leftover cake and cake layering scraps. Now, instead of committing to a whole slice of cake, you can get a bite or two or three.

You can choose to follow the recipe, or get crazy, without our guidance, using leftovers to concoct your own. Don't limit yourself to carrot cake; you can use any cake scrap and any leftover fillings, crumbs, or crunches. Chocolate Chip Cake (page 94) scraps with Fudge Sauce (page 136) and ground Peanut Brittle (page 169) couldn't be anything but a success.

The basics for cake truffles are as follows:

The base: Cake scraps, the fresher the better. We stick to one flavor of cake scraps at a time.

The binder: This can be the additional milky soak from a cake assembly or a moist filling, curd, or sauce. Depending on the moistness of the cake base, we use more or less binder. We have recipes, but there is always a range for the binder.

The shell: To seal in freshness and flavor, we roll each truffle in melted chocolate. The melted chocolate also serves to glue the crunchy coat onto the outside. We use Valrhona 72% dark chocolate or white chocolate, depending on the flavor of the cake truffle.

The crunchy coat: Finely ground crumbs or crunches work best, but we've even been known to use toasted yellow cake crumbs.

300 g	Carrot Cake scraps (page 119)	3 cups
25 to 50 g	Liquid Cheesecake (page 149)	2 to 4 tablespoons
½ recipe	Milk Crumb (page 74), finely ground in a food processor	
90 g	white chocolate, melted	3 ounces

1. Combine the carrot cake scraps and 25 g (2 tablespoons) liquid cheese-cake in the bowl of a stand mixer fitted with the paddle attachment and paddle until moist enough to knead into a ball. If it is not moist enough to do so, add up to 25 g (2 tablespoons) more liquid cheesecake and knead it in.

2. Using a soup spoon, portion out 12 even balls, each half the size of a Ping-Pong ball. Roll each one between the palms of your hands to shape and smooth it into a round sphere.

3. Put the ground milk crumbs in a medium bowl. With latex gloves on, put 2 tablespoons of the white chocolate in the palm of your hand and roll each ball between your palms, coating it in a thin layer of melted chocolate; add more chocolate as needed.

Steps 3 and 4 are easiest when you have a buddy: one person coats the cake balls in melted chocolate, the other tosses them in the milk crumbs.

4. Put 3 or 4 chocolate-covered balls at a time into the bowl of milk crumbs. Immediately toss them with the crumbs to coat, before the chocolate shell sets and no longer acts as a glue (if this happens, just coat the ball in another thin layer of melted chocolate).

5. Refrigerate for at least 5 minutes to fully set the chocolate shells before eating or storing. In an airtight container, the truffles will keep for up to 1 week in the fridge.

brownie pie

MAKES 1 (10-INCH) PIE; SERVES 8 TO 10

¾ recipe	Graham Crust (page 112)	255 g (1½ cups)
125 g	72% chocolate	4½ ounces
85 g	butter	6 tablespoons
2	eggs	
150 g	sugar	¾ cup
40 g	flour	¼ cup
25 g	cocoa powder, preferably Valrhona	3 tablespoons
2 g	kosher salt	½ teaspoon
110 g	heavy cream	½ cup

You can decorate the pie with a sprinkling of confectioners' sugar. To plate this pie with a VIP look, use a spoon or an offset spatula to smear a little Fudge Sauce (page 136) in a circle toward the center of the pie and garnish a small outer circle with Chocolate Crumbs (page 77).

1. Heat the oven to 350°F.

2. Dump 210 g (1¼ cups) graham crust into a 10-inch pie tin and set the remaining 45 g (¼ cup) to the side. With your fingers and the palms of your hands, press the crust firmly into the pie tin, covering the bottom and sides of the pan completely. Wrapped in plastic, the crust can be refrigerated or frozen for up to 2 weeks.

Warm the graham crust slightly in the microwave to make it easy to mold.

3. Combine the chocolate and butter in a microwave-safe bowl and gently melt them together on low for 30 to 50 seconds. Use a heatproof spatula to stir them together, working until the mixture is glossy and smooth.

4. Combine the eggs and sugar in the bowl of a stand mixer fitted with the whisk attachment and whip together on high for 3 to 4 minutes, until the mixture is fluffy and pale yellow and has reached the ribbon state. (Detach your whisk, dunk it into the whipped eggs, and wave it back and forth like a pendulum: the mixture should form a thickened, silky ribbon that falls and then disappears into the batter.) If the mixture does not form ribbons, continue whipping on high as needed.

5. Replace the whisk with the paddle attachment. Dump the chocolate mixture into the eggs and briefly mix together on low, then increase the speed to medium and paddle the mixture for 1 minute, or until it is brown and completely homogenous. If there are any dark streaks of chocolate, paddle for a few seconds longer, or as needed. Scrape down the sides of the bowl.

6. Add the flour, cocoa powder, and salt and paddle on low speed for 45 to 60 seconds. There should be no clumps of dry ingredients. If there are any lumps, mix for an additional 30 seconds. Scrape down the sides of the bowl.

7. Stream in the heavy cream on low speed, mixing for 30 to 45 seconds, just until the batter has loosened up a little and the white streaks of cream are fully mixed in. Scrape down the sides of the bowl.

8. Detach the paddle and remove the bowl from the mixer. Gently fold in the 45 g (¼ cup) graham crust with a spatula. (These crumbs will add little bursts of flavor and texture into the pie filling.)

9. Grab a sheet pan and put your pie tin of graham crust on it. With a spatula, scrape the brownie batter into the graham shell. Bake for 25 minutes. The pie should puff slightly on the sides and develop a sugary crust on top. If the brownie pie is still liquid in the center and has not formed a crust, bake it for an additional 5 minutes or so.

10. Cool the pie on a rack. (You can speed up the cooling process by carefully transferring the pie to the fridge or freezer directly out of the oven if you're in a hurry.) Wrapped in plastic, the pie will keep fresh in the fridge for up to 1 week or in the freezer for up to 2 weeks.

grasshopper pie

MAKES 1 (10-INCH) PIE; SERVES 8 TO 10

Our grasshopper pie is like a brownie pie that got drunk on crème de menthe.

1 recipe	Brownie Pie (page 124), prepared through step 8		
1 recipe	Mint Cheesecake Filling (recipe follows)		
20 g	mini chocolate chips	2 tablespoons	
25 g	mini marshmallows	½ cup	
1 recipe	Mint Glaze (recipe follows), warm		

You'll need less than a full recipe of brownie pie filling. Save the excess brownie batter that won't squeeze into the pie and bake it in cupcake molds!

1. Heat the oven to 350°F.

2. Grab a sheet pan and put your pie tin of graham crust on it. Pour the mint cheesecake filling into the shell. Pour the brownie batter on top of it. Use the tip of a knife to swirl the batter and mint filling, teasing up streaks of the mint filling so they show through the brownie batter.

3. Sprinkle the mini chocolate chips into a small ring in the center of the pie, leaving the bull's-eye center empty. Sprinkle the mini marshmallows into a ring around the ring of chocolate chips.

4. Bake the pie for 25 minutes. It should puff slightly on the edges but still be jiggly in the center. The mini chocolate chips will look as if they are beginning to melt, and the mini marshmallows should be evenly tanned. Leave the pie in the oven for an additional 3 to 4 minutes if this is not the case.

5. Cool the pie completely before finishing it. (You can speed up the cooling process by carefully transferring the pie to the fridge or freezer directly out of the oven if you're in a hurry.)

6. Now the pie needs to be Jackson-Pollocked with mint glaze. Make sure your glaze is still warm to the touch. Dunk the tines of a fork into the warm glaze, then dangle the fork about 1 inch above the bull's-eye center of the pie.

7. Transfer the pie to the fridge so the mint glaze firms up before serving—which will happen as soon as it's cold, about 15 minutes. Wrapped in plastic, the pie will keep fresh in the fridge for up to 1 week or in the freezer for up to 2 weeks.

mint cheesecake filling

MAKES ENOUGH FOR 1 GRASSHOPPER PIE

We tried, tried, tried to make this work with our liquid cheesecake—one of our mother recipes and one of my favorite things to eat and cook with—but the finished pie just wasn't right. So we came up with this work-around.

This filling is very deep in flavor and sweetness, only meant to be layered in a gooey brownie pie. Do not attempt to snack on it or use it in another recipe.

60 g	white chocolate	2 ounces
20 g	grapeseed oil	2 tablespoons
75 g	cream cheese	2½ ounces
20 g	confectioners' sugar	2 tablespoons
2 g	peppermint extract	½ teaspoon
1 g	kosher salt	¼ teaspoon
2 drops	green food coloring	

1. Combine the white chocolate and oil in a microwave-safe dish and gently melt the mixture on low for 30 to 50 seconds. Use a heatproof spatula to stir the chocolate and oil together, working until the mixture is glossy and smooth.

2. Combine the cream cheese and confectioners' sugar in the bowl of a stand mixer fitted with the paddle attachment and stir together on medium-low speed for 2 to 3 minutes to blend. Scrape down the sides of the bowl.

3. On low speed, slowly stream in the white chocolate mixture. Mix for 1 to 2 minutes, until it is fully incorporated into the cream cheese. Scrape down the sides of the bowl.

4. Add the peppermint extract, salt, and food coloring and paddle the mixture for 1 to 2 minutes, or just until it is smooth and leprechaun green. (You may need to scrape the bowl down once midmixing.) No point in making ahead— you don't have any use for it otherwise and it will make it trickier to swirl in later.

mint glaze

MAKES ENOUGH FOR 1 GRASSHOPPER PIE

Make this glaze just before using it—it needs to be warm so that you can properly make a mess of the top of a pie with it.

30 g	white chocolate	1 ounce
6 g	grapeseed oil	2 teaspoons
0.5 g	peppermint extract	scant ⅛ teaspoon
1 drop	green food coloring	

1. Combine the white chocolate and oil in a microwave-safe dish and melt the chocolate on low for 20 to 30 seconds. Use a heatproof spatula to stir the oil and chocolate together, working until the mixture is glossy and smooth.

2. Stir in the peppermint extract and food coloring.

white peach sorbet
graham puree, milk crumbs

SERVES 4

This was one of the first spring desserts we made for Ko. It is simple but somehow hits home in just the right way.

1 recipe	Graham Ganache (recipe follows)
1 recipe	White Peach Sorbet (recipe follows)
½ recipe	Milk Crumb (page 74)

Use the back of a spoon to schmear (see page 29) a quarter of the graham ganache into each of 4 bowls. Make quenelles (see page 28) or scoops of sorbet and set 1 in the center of each schmeared bowl. Sprinkle the milk crumbs over and around the sorbet. Serve at once.

graham ganache

MAKES ABOUT 150 G (⅓ CUP)

½ recipe	Graham Crust (page 112)		
85 g	milk	⅓ cup	
2 g	kosher salt	½ teaspoon	

Combine the graham crust, milk, and salt in a blender and puree on medium speed until smooth and homogenous—it will take 1 to 3 minutes (depending on the awesomeness of your blender). If the mixture does not catch on your blender blade, turn it off, take a small teaspoon, and scrape down the sides of the canister, remembering to scrape under the blade, then try again. Use the ganache right away, or store in an airtight container in the fridge for up to 5 days.

white peach sorbet

MAKES ABOUT 450 G (1 PINT)

400 g	ripe white peaches	about 5
1	gelatin sheet	
100 g	glucose	¼ cup
2 g	kosher salt	½ teaspoon
0.5 g	citric acid (see page 16)	⅛ teaspoon

1. Cut the peaches in half and pit them. Plop them into a blender and puree until smooth and homogenous, 1 to 3 minutes. Pass the puree through a fine-mesh sieve into a medium bowl. Use a ladle or spoon to press on the dregs of the puree to extract as much juice as possible; you should only be discarding a few spoonfuls worth of solids.

2. Bloom the gelatin (see page 29).

3. Warm a little bit of the peach puree and whisk in the gelatin to dissolve. Whisk in the remaining peach puree, the glucose, salt, and citric acid until everything is fully dissolved and incorporated.

4. Pour the mixture into your ice cream machine and freeze according to the manufacturer's instructions. The sorbet is best spun just before serving or using, but it will keep in an airtight container in the freezer for up to 2 weeks.

Powdered gelatin can be substituted for the sheet gelatin: use ½ teaspoon. In a pinch, substitute 35 g (2 tablespoons) corn syrup for the glucose.

With all things fresh and seasonal, it's always important to taste, taste, taste. Make the sorbet base to your liking with more glucose, salt, or citric acid (see page 26).

Instead of a whisk, use a hand blender to mix the sorbet base.

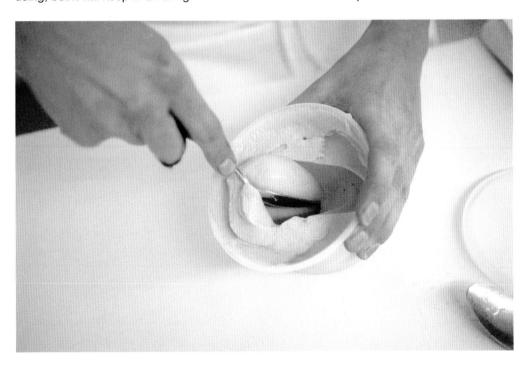

fudge sauce

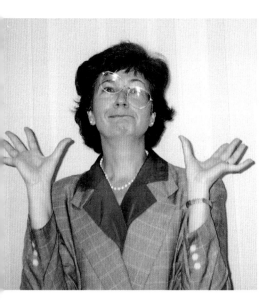

My mother is a hot fudge fanatic. An insane, uncritical fanatic. Because of her, I think of fudge sauce as (1) Hershey's Chocolate Syrup, which was a fixture at our house, or (2) what they use at McDonald's, where my stepdad regularly takes my mom on $1.50 sundae dates.

It was a no-brainer that we'd need a fudge sauce for Milk Bar. But I didn't learn how to make trashy American fudge sauce at the French Culinary Institute, and I didn't want to have to decode the chemist's secrets behind Hershey's Syrup, or the more lavish Chocolate Shell (which was too fancy for our house), in order to put chocolate sauce on my ice cream cones.

So I threw myself into it. I wanted the sauce fudgy and I wanted it shiny. We frosted my favorite chocolate cake at culinary school with a ridiculously shiny chocolate glaze, and for some reason, that shininess always wooed me.

I started mixing chocolate and cocoa powder, sugar, and heavy cream—just like they teach you in school. I added salt to taste, and then I began to add glucose—liquid sugar, liquid shine. Whisk, whisk. Not shiny enough. More glucose. Whisk. Not thick enough, not shiny enough. More glucose. Taste. Never shiny enough, never quite the right thickness or body. Marian rolled her eyes.

After you taste something too many times in a row, you get tunnel vision and can't judge it fairly. I stopped after I had added more glucose than heavy cream and could no longer really taste the sauce.

The next day, Marian and I—sure we had a couple of diligent days of testing ahead of us to nail it—went to taste the sauce. Then we looked at each other over our morning coffees and knew we *had* it.

The recipe has never changed; there are clearly no real secret ingredients in it. But somehow this recipe became the secret ingredient itself. It is so damn good that we throw it into almost everything chocolate-based to give it a bump of chocolatiness that seems otherwise impossible to achieve. We fold it into cake batters, schmear it on plates for composed desserts, and buzz it into ice cream bases. And we pour it over sundaes for family meal.

fudge sauce

MAKES ABOUT 150 G (½ CUP), OR ENOUGH FOR 4 OR MORE SUNDAES

30 g	72% chocolate, chopped	1 ounce
18 g	cocoa powder, preferably Valrhona	2 tablespoons
0.5 g	kosher salt	⅛ teaspoon
100 g	glucose	¼ cup
25 g	sugar	2 tablespoons
55 g	heavy cream	¼ cup

In a pinch, substitute 35 g (2 tablespoons) corn syrup for the glucose.

1. Combine the chocolate, cocoa powder, and salt in a medium bowl.

2. Combine the glucose, sugar, and heavy cream in a heavy-bottomed saucepan and stir intermittently while bringing to a boil over high heat. The moment it boils, pour it into the bowl holding the chocolate. Let sit for 1 full minute.

3. Slowly, slowly begin to whisk the mixture. Then continue, increasing the vigor of your whisking every 30 seconds, until the mixture is glossy and silky-smooth. This will take 2 to 4 minutes, depending on your speed and strength. You can use the sauce at this point or store it in an airtight container in the fridge for up to 2 weeks; do not freeze.

Elsewhere in this book: Fudge sauce is used for a fancier presentation of the Brownie Pie (page 124).

hot fudge sauce

Our fudge sauce tastes just as good hot as it does cold. Simply warm it in the microwave on low in 30-second increments for 2 minutes. Stir the sauce between blasts. It tastes really good drizzled over Cereal Milk Ice Cream (page 38). Or any ice cream, for that matter. My mother approves.

malt fudge sauce

MAKES ABOUT 450 G (1¾ CUPS), OR ENOUGH FOR 12 OR MORE SUNDAES

I wasn't raised on malt as a flavor, but as we expanded our little kitchen staff, Leslie Behrens opened us up to a world of malt. After many attempts at this sauce, we found the secret to a deep, dark underlying malt flavor is a splash of molasses—not enough to taste molasses, but enough to give a deep, dark depth beyond chocolate alone.

60 g	72% chocolate, chopped	2 ounces	
80 g	Ovaltine, malt flavor	1 cup	
5 g	molasses	1 teaspoon	Substitute any dark cane syrup for the molasses.
1 g	kosher salt	¼ teaspoon	
200 g	glucose	½ cup	In a pinch, substitute 35 g (2 tablespoons) corn syrup for the glucose.
50 g	sugar	¼ cup	
110 g	heavy cream	½ cup	

Follow the recipe for the fudge sauce, substituting the Ovaltine for the cocoa powder and adding the molasses along with it.

earl grey fudge sauce

MAKES ABOUT 250 G (⅔ CUP), OR ENOUGH FOR 4 OR MORE SUNDAES

This is our high-brow fudge sauce for the Earl Grey lovers out there (Mama Meehan, we're looking at you).

40 g	water	3 tablespoons
1	Earl Grey tea bag	
30 g	72% chocolate, chopped	1 ounce
18 g	cocoa powder, preferably Valrhona	2 tablespoons
0.5 g	kosher salt	⅛ teaspoon
100 g	glucose	¼ cup
25 g	sugar	2 tablespoons
55 g	heavy cream	¼ cup

In a pinch, substitute 35 g (2 tablespoons) corn syrup for the glucose.

1. Bring the water to a boil in a small saucepan or in a tea cup in the microwave. Remove from heat, add the tea, and let steep for 4 minutes.

2. Wring and remove the tea bag and pour the tea into a medium bowl. Add the chocolate, cocoa powder, and salt.

3. Combine the glucose, sugar, and heavy cream in a heavy-bottomed saucepan and stir intermittently while bringing to a boil over high heat. The moment it boils, pour it into the bowl holding the chocolate. Let sit for 1 full minute.

4. Slowly, slowly begin to whisk the mixture. Then continue, increasing the vigor of your whisking every 30 seconds, until the mixture is glossy and silky-smooth. This will take 2 to 4 minutes, depending on your speed and strength. You can use the sauce at this point or store it in an airtight container in the fridge for up to 2 weeks; do not freeze.

chocolate malt layer cake

MAKES 1 (6-INCH) LAYER CAKE, 5 TO 6 INCHES TALL; SERVES 6 TO 8

1 recipe	Chocolate Cake (recipe follows)
1 recipe	Ovaltine Soak (recipe follows)
1 recipe	Malt Fudge Sauce (page 137), warm
½ recipe	Malted Milk Crumb (page 76)
1 recipe	Charred Marshmallows (recipe follows)

special equipment

1 (6-inch) cake ring

2 strips acetate, each 3 inches wide and 20 inches long

1. Put a piece of parchment or a Silpat on the counter. Invert the cake onto it and peel off the parchment or Silpat from the bottom of the cake. Use the cake ring to stamp out 2 circles from the cake. These are your top 2 cake layers. The remaining cake "scrap" will come together to make the bottom layer of the cake.

layer 1, the bottom
2. Clean the cake ring and place it in the center of a sheet pan lined with clean parchment or a Silpat. Use 1 strip of acetate to line the inside of the cake ring.

3. Put the cake scraps inside the ring and use the back of your hand to tamp the scraps together into a flat even layer.

4. Dunk a pastry brush in the Ovaltine soak and give the layer of cake a good, healthy bath of half of the soak.

5. Use the back of a spoon to spread one-fifth of the malt fudge sauce in an even layer over the cake. (Helpful hint: the warmer the fudge sauce, the easier it is to spread.)

6. Sprinkle half of the malted milk crumbs and one-third of the charred marshmallows evenly over the malt fudge sauce. Use the back of your hand to anchor them in place.

7. Use the back of a spoon to spread another fifth of the malt fudge sauce as evenly as possible over the crumbs and marshmallows.

recipe continues

layer 2, the middle

8. With your index finger, gently tuck the second strip of acetate between the cake ring and the top ¼ inch of the first strip of acetate, so that you have a clear ring of acetate 5 to 6 inches tall—high enough to support the height of the finished cake. Set a cake round on top of the sauce and repeat the process for layer 1 (if 1 of your 2 cake rounds is jankier than the other, use it here in the middle and save the prettier one for the top).

layer 3, the top

9. Nestle the remaining cake round into the sauce. Cover the top of the cake with the remaining fudge sauce. Since it's a sauce, not a frosting, here you have no choice but to make a shiny, perfectly flat top. Garnish with the remaining charred marshmallows.

10. Transfer the sheet pan to the freezer and freeze for a minimum of 12 hours to set the cake and filling. The cake will keep in the freezer for up to 2 weeks.

11. At least 3 hours before you are ready to serve the cake, pull the sheet pan out of the freezer and, using your fingers and thumbs, pop the cake out of the cake ring. Gently peel off the acetate and transfer the cake to a platter or cake stand. Let it defrost in the fridge for a minimum of 3 hours. If storing the cake for longer, do *not* cover with plastic wrap—it will tear the malt fudge off the cake! Instead, get a big bowl, flip it upside down, and use it to protect the cake (or invest in a cake carrier). Stored in this way, the cake will keep fresh for up to 5 days in the fridge.

12. Slice the cake into wedges and serve.

chocolate cake

MAKES 1 QUARTER SHEET PAN CAKE

115 g	butter, at room temperature	8 tablespoons (1 stick)
300 g	sugar	1½ cups
3	eggs	
110 g	buttermilk	½ cup
40 g	grapeseed oil	¼ cup
4 g	vanilla extract	1 teaspoon
¼ recipe	Fudge Sauce (page 136)	38 g (3 tablespoons)
155 g	cake flour	1¼ cups
70 g	cocoa powder, preferably Valrhona	½ cup
6 g	baking powder	1½ teaspoons
6 g	kosher salt	1½ teaspoons
	Pam or other nonstick cooking spray (optional)	

1. Heat the oven to 350°F.

2. Combine the butter and sugar in the bowl of a stand mixer fitted with the paddle attachment and cream together on medium-high for 2 to 3 minutes. Scrape down the sides of the bowl, add the eggs, and mix on medium-high for 2 to 3 minutes. Scrape down the sides of the bowl once more.

3. On low speed, stream in the buttermilk, oil, and vanilla. Increase the mixer speed to medium-high and paddle for 3 to 5 minutes, until the mixture is practically white, twice the size of your original fluffy butter-and-sugar mixture, and completely homogenous. There should be no streaks of fat or liquid. Stop the mixer and scrape down the sides of the bowl.

4. Add the fudge sauce and mix on low speed until fully incorporated. Scrape down the sides of the bowl.

5. With a spatula, stir the flour, cocoa powder, baking powder, and salt together in a medium bowl. On very low speed, add the dry ingredients and mix for 45 to 60 seconds, just until your batter comes together. Scrape down the sides of the bowl, and mix on low speed for another 45 seconds to ensure that any little lumps of cocoa powder and cake flour are incorporated.

recipe continues

6. Pam-spray a quarter sheet pan and line it with parchment, or just line the pan with a Silpat. Using a spatula, spread the cake batter in an even layer in the pan. Bake for 30 to 35 minutes. The cake will rise and puff, doubling in size, but will remain slightly buttery and dense. At 30 minutes, gently poke the edge of the cake with your finger: the cake should bounce back slightly and the center should no longer be jiggly. Leave the cake in the oven for an extra 3 to 5 minutes if it doesn't pass these tests.

7. Take the cake out of the oven and cool on a wire rack or, in a pinch, in the fridge or freezer (don't worry, it's not cheating). The cooled cake can be stored, wrapped in plastic wrap, for up to 5 days.

ovaltine soak

MAKES ABOUT 65 G (¼ CUP)

55 g	milk	¼ cup	
10 g	Ovaltine, malt flavor	2 tablespoons	

Whisk together the milk and Ovaltine in a small bowl until the Ovaltine is completely dissolved. Use immediately.

charred marshmallows

MAKES ABOUT 150 G (2¾ CUPS)

The only thing we really use our blow-torch for is to char these marshmallows. If you or your significant other happens to be a handy person, then perhaps you already have one. If not, you should get one, because they are superfun to play with and you can teach yourself to weld. That said, it's not necessary to go out and buy one: you can char the marshmallows under the broiler of your oven or any other type of open flame—like a wand lighter.

I light a forest fire on my sheet pan of mini marshmallows and let it burn out on its own. The surface of all the marshmallows should be black/burnt, while the bottoms remain perfectly white.

150 g	mini marshmallows	2¾ cups	

Spread the marshmallows out evenly on an unlined sheet pan and char them to hell and back with a blowtorch. Transfer the pan to the fridge or freezer for 10 minutes to firm up the marshmallows and make them easier to handle. Use immediately or store in an airtight container at room temperature for up to 1 week.

red velvet ice cream

MAKES ABOUT 450 G (1 PINT)

We use cake scraps in our kitchen for just about anything. Really. Even ice creams, where they add body, texture, and depth of flavor. We put chocolate cake scraps in the red velvet ice cream because we want it to taste like red velvet cake. We also like to take it too far and swirl red velvet ice cream with cream cheese frosting ice cream.

1	gelatin sheet	
220 g	milk	1 cup
½ recipe	Fudge Sauce (page 136)	
50 g	Chocolate Cake "scraps" (page 141)	½ cup
35 g	cocoa powder, preferably Valrhona	¼ cup
25 g	sugar	2 tablespoons
25 g	glucose	1 tablespoon
12 g	distilled white vinegar	1 tablespoon
12 g	buttermilk	1 tablespoon
8 g	red food coloring	2 teaspoons
4 g	kosher salt	1 teaspoon

Powdered gelatin can be substituted for the sheet gelatin: use ½ teaspoon. In a pinch, substitute 9 g (2 teaspoons) corn syrup for the glucose.

1. Bloom the gelatin (see page 29).

2. Warm a little bit of the milk and whisk in the gelatin to dissolve. Transfer the gelatin mixture to a blender, add the remaining milk, the fudge sauce, chocolate cake, cocoa powder, sugar, glucose, vinegar, buttermilk, food coloring, and salt, and puree until smooth and even. Don't be stingy on the blending time—the cake scraps need to soak up the liquid and kind of dissipate into the mixture.

3. Pour the mixture through a fine-mesh sieve into your ice cream machine and freeze according to the manufacturer's instructions. The ice cream is best spun just before serving or using, but it will keep in an airtight container in the freezer for up to 2 weeks.

liquid

cheesecake

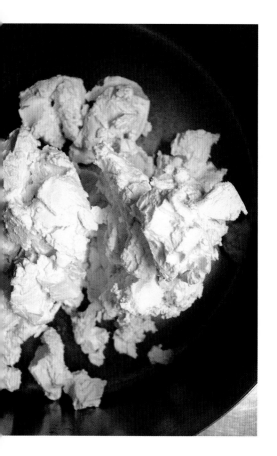

Back to my childhood obsession with Jell-O No-Bake Cheesecake. . . . Once I trashed the graham crust, I'd dine on the filling. I'd whisk the powdered cheesecake mixture into some milk and watch it thicken and magically transform itself, no heat required. I'd go over to my friend Megan's house to mix and eat it because her mom wouldn't stop me (she'd just look on, horrified) as I fed myself an entire pie's worth of thickened, creamy cheesecake-like filling. Mmmmm.

In case you haven't figured it out, I'm kind of a fan of the gooey, just-barely-baked approach to making something delicious. There's something so naughty and fulfilling about the texture. I'm sure a psychiatrist would tell me it's because I was deprived of cookie dough for so long (cough, thanks, Mom, cough).

When I worked at wd~50, we would make the most deliciously rich cheesecakes with unlikely cheeses like Manchego, the semi-firm aged Spanish sheep's-milk cheese, and Cabrales, the stinky firm blue cheese made from the milk of Spanish cows. When Sam, the pastry chef, wasn't looking or was busy during service, I would shamelessly scrape some batter from the bowl into a pint container and either eat the batter raw or warm it slightly in the microwave to get it to barely set. Sometimes I ate so much of it that I'd have to make more for service.

Once I'd settled into my role as pastry chef at Momofuku, I knew I had every right to eat magically thickened cheesecake filling in the confines of my new home. But I also knew I had to develop my own take on many of the beloved staples of my diet, and so began the search for my voice in the form of cheesecake.

It was a short journey: my heart beats for one and only one kind of cheesecake—the underbaked, messy kind. And so, my signature cheese-cake is liquid cheesecake.

liquid cheesecake

MAKES ABOUT 325 G (1½ CUPS)

225 g	cream cheese	8 ounces
150 g	sugar	¾ cup
6 g	cornstarch	1 tablespoon
2 g	kosher salt	½ teaspoon
25 g	milk	2 tablespoons
1	egg	

1. Heat the oven to 300°F.

2. Put the cream cheese in the bowl of a stand mixer fitted with the paddle attachment and mix on low speed for 2 minutes. Scrape down the sides of the bowl with a spatula. Add the sugar and mix for 1 to 2 minutes, until the sugar has been completely incorporated. Scrape down the sides of the bowl.

3. Whisk together the cornstarch and salt in a medium bowl. Whisk in the milk in a slow, steady stream, then whisk in the egg until the slurry is homogenous.

4. With the mixer on medium-low speed, stream in the egg slurry. Paddle for 3 to 4 minutes, until the mixture is smooth and loose. Scrape down the sides of the bowl.

5. Line the bottom and sides of a 6 × 6-inch baking pan with plastic wrap. Pour the cheesecake batter into the pan, put the pan in the oven, and bake for 15 minutes. Gently shake the pan. The cheesecake should be firmer and more set toward the outer boundaries of the baking pan but still be jiggly and loose in the dead center. If the cheesecake is jiggly all over, give it 5 minutes more. And 5 minutes more if it needs it, but it's never taken me more than 25 minutes to underbake one. If the cheesecake rises more than a ¼ inch or begins to brown, take it out of the oven immediately.

6. Cool the cheesecake completely, to finish the baking process and allow the cheesecake to set. The final product will resemble a cheesecake, but it will be pipeable and pliable enough to easily spread or smear, while still having body and volume. Once cool, the cheesecake can be stored in an airtight container in the fridge for up to 1 week.

Elsewhere in this book: Liquid cheesecake is used in the Carrot Layer Cake (page 117).

cheesecake ice cream

MAKES ABOUT 450 G (1 PINT)

At our East Village Milk Bar, we have two big-boy soft-serve machines that churn ice cream day and night. To keep ourselves entertained and to keep customers interested, we change the flavors every six weeks, basing each flight of flavors around a theme. This recipe was part of a suite of ice creams flavored liked baked goods, and, true to its name, it tastes just like cheesecake. The twist with it and our key lime pie ice cream was crazy good!

1	gelatin sheet	
220 g	milk	1 cup
½ recipe	Liquid Cheesecake (page 149)	
15 g	sour cream	1 tablespoon
¼ recipe	Graham Crust (page 112)	85 g (½ cup)
20 g	milk powder	¼ cup
2 g	kosher salt	½ teaspoon

Powdered gelatin can be substituted for the sheet gelatin: use ½ teaspoon.

1. Bloom the gelatin (see page 29).

2. Warm a little bit of the milk and whisk in the gelatin to dissolve.

3. Transfer the gelatin mixture to a blender, add the remaining milk, the liquid cheesecake, sour cream, graham crust, milk powder, and salt, and puree until smooth and even. Don't be stingy on the blending time: you want to make sure the graham crust is completely liquefied; otherwise, your cheesecake ice cream will be missing that flavor.

4. Pour the ice cream base through a fine-mesh sieve into your ice cream machine and freeze according to the manufacturer's instructions. The ice cream is best spun just before serving or using, but it will keep in an airtight container in the freezer for up to 2 weeks.

cinnamon bun pie

MAKES 1 (10-INCH) PIE; SERVES 8 TO 10

While I tried to have the recipes in this book build chapter-by-chapter on those that came before, sometimes that wasn't possible. So jump ahead and read about the mother dough (page 218) before you get going on this pie.

When we first opened Milk Bar, at 4 or 5 o'clock every morning we would make fresh cinnamon buns with liquid cheesecake rolled up into the dough instead of applying cream cheese frosting on top. Cinnamon buns are something I feel very strongly about, since my mother started a tradition of making (not-so-great) ones for breakfast on every holiday. (Sorry, Mom, but you can't give a kid a Cinnabon and then expect her to be OK with cinnamon buns made with margarine and skim milk!) We'd make them before the crack of dawn so they'd be ready for breakfast . . . and then we'd sell most of them to people on their way home at night, ready to tuck in with dessert and some TV. So we decided to get smart and create something that was delicious, available, and fresh at any hour, and didn't have to be made to order every morning: the cinnamon bun pie.

½ recipe	Mother Dough (page 222), proofed	
30 g	flour, for dusting	3 tablespoons
80 g	brown butter (see page 28)	¼ cup
1 recipe	Liquid Cheesecake (page 149)	
60 g	light brown sugar	¼ cup tightly packed
1 g	kosher salt	¼ teaspoon
2 g	ground cinnamon	1 teaspoon
1 recipe	Cinnamon Streusel (recipe follows)	

1. Heat the oven to 350°F.

2. Punch down and flatten the proofed dough.

3. Take a pinch of flour and throw it across the surface of a smooth dry countertop as if you were skipping a rock on water, to lightly coat the counter. Take another pinch of flour and lightly dust a rolling pin. Use the rolling pin to flatten the punched-down circle of dough, then roll out the dough with the rolling pin or stretch the dough out by hand as if you were making a pizza from scratch. Your end goal is to create a large circle that is approximately

recipe continues

11 inches in diameter. Keep your 10-inch pie tin nearby for reference. The 11-inch dough round should be ¼ to ½ inch thick.

4. Gently place the dough in the pie tin. Alternate between using your fingers and palms of your hands to press the dough firmly into place. Put the pie tin on a sheet pan.

5. Use the back of a spoon to spread half of the brown butter in an even layer over the dough.

6. Use the back of another spoon (you don't want brown butter in your creamy white cheesecake layer!) to spread half the liquid cheesecake in an even layer over the brown butter. Spread the remaining brown butter in an even layer over the liquid cheesecake.

7. Scatter the brown sugar on top of the brown butter. Tamp it down with the back of your hand to help keep it in place. Then sprinkle evenly with the salt and cinnamon.

8. Now for the trickiest layer: the remaining liquid cheesecake. Stay cool, and spread it as gently as you can to achieve the most even layer possible.

9. Sprinkle the streusel evenly on top of the cheesecake layer. Use the back of your hand to secure the streusel.

10. Bake the pie for 40 minutes. The crust will puff and brown, the liquid cheesecake will set firm, and the streusel topping will crunch up and brown. After 40 minutes, gently shake the pan. The center of the pie should be slightly jiggly. The filling should be set toward the outer boundaries of the pie tin. If some of the filling erupted onto the sheet pan below, don't worry—consider it a snack for later. If necessary, bake for an additional 5 minutes, until the pie meets the description above.

11. Cool the pie on a wire rack. To store, cool the pie completely and wrap well in plastic wrap. In the fridge, the pie will keep fresh for 3 days (the crust gets stale quickly); in the freezer, it will keep for 1 month.

12. When you are ready to serve the pie, know that it's best served warm! Slice and microwave each slice on high for 30 seconds, or warm the whole pie in a 250°F oven for 10 to 20 minutes, then slice and serve.

cinnamon streusel

MAKES ABOUT 120 G (⅔ CUP)

40 g	flour	¼ cup
20 g	old-fashioned rolled oats	¼ cup
2 g	ground cinnamon	1 teaspoon
1 g	kosher salt	¼ teaspoon
30 g	light brown sugar	2 tablespoons
25 g	butter, melted	2 tablespoons
0.5 g	vanilla extract	⅛ teaspoon

1. In a bowl combine the flour, oats, cinnamon, salt, and brown sugar with a spoon or spatula until the dry ingredients are incorporated. Pour in the melted butter and vanilla and toss the mixture until almond-size dark oat clusters form.

2. If you're making the pie the same day, the streusel can wait out on the counter. If you're making the streusel in advance, transfer it to an airtight container and store in the fridge or freezer for up to 2 weeks.

apple pie layer cake

MAKES 1 (6-INCH) LAYER CAKE, 5 TO 6 INCHES TALL; SERVES 6 TO 8

When we opened Ko, we did so with a deep-fried apple pie. It resonated so much with people that we decided to use the apple pie as inspiration for a cake. We already had the crumb-into-ganache-into-frosting down and we loved the pie crumb we had developed for a few Noodle Bar and Ko desserts seasons before.

This cake will make you seem like a genius, though all you are doing is layering apple pie fixins between layers of slightly nutty (with brown butter) cake. Leftovers make especially delicious impromptu cake truffles (see page 122).

1 recipe	Barely Brown Butter Cake (recipe follows)	
1 recipe	Apple Cider Soak (recipe follows)	
1 recipe	Liquid Cheesecake (page 149)	
½ recipe	Pie Crumb (page 79)	
1 recipe	Apple Pie Filling (recipe follows)	
½ recipe	Pie Crumb Frosting (recipe follows)	

special equipment

1 (6-inch) cake ring

2 strips acetate, each 3 inches wide and 20 inches long

1. Put a piece of parchment or a Silpat on the counter. Invert the cake onto it and peel off the parchment or Silpat from the bottom of the cake. Use the cake ring to stamp out 2 circles from the cake. These are your top 2 cake layers. The remaining cake "scrap" will come together to make the bottom layer of the cake.

layer 1, the bottom
2. Clean the cake ring and place it in the center of a sheet pan lined with clean parchment or a Silpat. Use 1 strip of acetate to line the inside of the cake ring.

3. Put the cake scraps inside the ring and use the back of your hand to tamp the scraps together into a flat even layer.

4. Dunk a pastry brush in the apple cider soak and give the layer of cake a good, healthy bath of half of the soak.

recipe continues

5. Use the back of a spoon to spread half of the liquid cheesecake in an even layer over the cake.

6. Sprinkle one-third of the pie crumbs evenly over the liquid cheesecake. Use the back of your hand to anchor them in place.

7. Use the back of a spoon to spread one-half of the apple pie filling as evenly as possible over the crumbs.

layer 2, the middle
8. With your index finger, gently tuck the second strip of acetate between the cake ring and the top ¼ inch of the first strip of acetate, so that you have a clear ring of acetate 5 to 6 inches tall—high enough to support the height of the finished cake. Set a cake round on top of the filling and repeat the process for layer 1 (if 1 of your 2 cake rounds is jankier than the other, use it here in the middle and save the prettier one for the top).

layer 3, the top
9. Nestle the remaining cake round into the apple pie filling. Cover the top of the cake with all of the pie crumb frosting. Give it volume and swirls, or do as we do and opt for a perfectly flat top. Garnish the frosting with the remaining pie crumbs.

10. Transfer the sheet pan to the freezer and freeze for a minimum of 12 hours to set the cake and filling. The cake will keep in the freezer for up to 2 weeks.

11. At least 3 hours before you are ready to serve the cake, pull the sheet pan out of the freezer and, using your fingers and thumbs, pop the cake out of the cake ring. Gently peel off the acetate and transfer the cake to a platter or cake stand. Let it defrost in the fridge for a minimum of 3 hours (wrapped well in plastic, it can be refrigerated for up to 5 days).

12. Slice the cake into wedges and serve.

barely brown butter cake

MAKES 1 QUARTER SHEET PAN

55 g	butter	4 tablespoons (½ stick)
40 g	brown butter (see page 28)	2 tablespoons
250 g	granulated sugar	1¼ cups
60 g	light brown sugar	¼ cup tightly packed
3	eggs	
110 g	buttermilk	½ cup
65 g	grapeseed oil	⅓ cup
2 g	vanilla extract	½ teaspoon
185 g	cake flour	1½ cups
4 g	baking powder	1 teaspoon
4 g	kosher salt	1 teaspoon
	Pam or other nonstick cooking spray (optional)	

There is a *ton* of liquid and fat in this amazing cake! If you do not do your due diligence to make sure that the batter is homogenous at each step (no streaks, discolorations, or other signs of separation/unincorporation), you'll be sorry when your cake bakes out of its pan and all over the bottom of your oven.

1. Heat the oven to 350°F.

2. Combine the butters and sugars in the bowl of a stand mixer fitted with the paddle attachment and cream together on medium-high for 2 to 3 minutes. Scrape down the sides of the bowl, add the eggs, and mix on medium-high for 2 to 3 minutes. Scrape down the sides of the bowl once more.

3. Stream in the buttermilk, oil, and vanilla while the paddle swirls on low speed. Increase the speed to medium-high and paddle 5 to 6 minutes, until the mixture is practically white, twice the size of your original fluffy butter-and-sugar mixture, and completely homogenous. You're basically forcing too much liquid into an already fatty mixture that doesn't want to make room for it, so if it doesn't look right after 6 minutes, keep mixing. Stop the mixer and scrape down the sides of the bowl.

4. On very low speed, add the cake flour, baking powder, and salt. Mix for 45 to 60 seconds, just until your batter comes together and any remnants of dry ingredients have been incorporated. Scrape down the sides of the bowl. Mix on low speed for another 45 seconds to ensure that any little lumps of cake flour are incorporated.

5. Pam-spray a quarter sheet pan and line it with parchment, or just line the pan with a Silpat. Using a spatula, spread the cake batter in an even layer in the pan. Bake for 30 to 35 minutes. The cake will rise and puff, doubling in

recipe continues

size, but will remain slightly buttery and dense. At 30 minutes, gently poke the edge of the cake with your finger: the cake should bounce back slightly and the center should no longer be jiggly. Leave the cake in the oven for an extra 3 to 5 minutes if it doesn't pass these tests.

6. Take the cake out of the oven and cool on a wire rack or, in a pinch, in the fridge or freezer (don't worry, it's not cheating). The cooled cake can be stored in the fridge, wrapped in plastic wrap, for up to 5 days.

apple cider soak

MAKES ABOUT 60 G (¼ CUP)

55 g	apple cider	¼ cup
5 g	light brown sugar	1 teaspoon tightly packed
0.25 g	ground cinnamon	pinch

Whisk together the cider, brown sugar, and cinnamon in a small bowl until the sugar is completely dissolved.

apple pie filling

MAKES ABOUT 400 G (1¾ CUPS)

1	lemon	
300 g	Granny Smith apples	2 medium
14 g	butter	1 tablespoon
150 g	light brown sugar	⅔ cup tightly packed
1 g	ground cinnamon	½ teaspoon
1 g	kosher salt	¼ teaspoon

1. Fill a medium bowl halfway with cold tap water. Juice the lemon into it. Fish out and discard any seeds. You will use this lemon water to keep your apple pieces looking fresh and pert.

2. Peel the apples, then halve and quarter them. Put each apple quarter on its side and cut a small slice down the length of the apple to remove the seeds and core. Cut each apple quarter lengthwise into thirds and then crosswise into fourths, leaving you with 12 small pieces from every apple quarter. Transfer these pieces to the lemon water as you go.

recipe continues

3. When you're ready to cook, drain the apples (discard the lemon water) and combine them in a medium pot with the butter, brown sugar, cinnamon, and salt. Slowly bring to a boil over medium heat, using a spoon to gently stir the mixture as it heats up and the apples begin to release liquid. Reduce the heat and simmer the apples gently for 3 to 5 minutes. Be careful not to cook the apples so much that they turn into applesauce.

4. Transfer to a container and put in the fridge to cool down. Once completely cooled, the filling can be stored in the fridge in an airtight container for up to 1 week; do not freeze.

pie crumb frosting

MAKES ABOUT 220 G (¾ CUP), OR ENOUGH FOR 2 APPLE PIE LAYER CAKES

½ recipe	Pie Crumb (page 79)	
110 g	milk	½ cup
2 g	kosher salt	½ teaspoon
40 g	butter, at room temperature	3 tablespoons
40 g	confectioners' sugar	¼ cup

It's hard to make pie crumb frosting in a smaller batch. So make this and dip some apple slices in the extra frosting for a quick snack.

1. Combine the pie crumbs, milk, and salt in a blender, turn the speed to medium-high, and puree until smooth and homogenous. It will take 1 to 3 minutes (depending on the awesomeness of your blender). If the mixture does not catch on your blender blade, turn off the blender, take a small teaspoon, and scrape down the sides of the canister, remembering to scrape under the blade, then try again.

2. Combine the butter and confectioners' sugar in the bowl of a stand mixer fitted with the paddle attachment and cream together on medium-high for 2 to 3 minutes, until fluffy and pale yellow. Scrape down the sides of the bowl with a spatula.

3. On low speed, paddle in the contents of the blender. After 1 minute, crank the speed up to medium-high and let her rip for another 2 minutes. Scrape down the sides of the bowl. If the mixture is not a uniform, very pale, barely tan color, give the bowl another scrape-down and another minute of high-speed paddling.

4. Use the frosting immediately, or store it in an airtight container in the fridge for up to 1 week.

guava sorbet
liquid cheesecake,
cream cheese skin

SERVES 4

When I moved to NYC to attend cooking school, I dove right in. I got several part-time jobs in a variety of locales. Basically, I worked for anyone who would hire me. Early morning. Late night. Magnolia Bakery didn't bite, but there was a bakery (now closed) in the West Village off Jane Street, run by a fiery Cuban woman who agreed to put me on the schedule.

After a late night of work as a hostess, I would drag myself in early the next morning to this strange bakery, almost the only motivation being a *pastelito,* a Cuban puff pastry topped with cane sugar and filled with guava paste and cream cheese. It was the most delicious and different pastry I had ever tasted, and I knew I'd want to use the flavor combo one day.

One time, when we were changing the menu at Ko and I was on a breakfast-inspired kick (guava and cream cheese is a classic breakfast pairing in many Spanish-speaking cultures), an idea took hold. I knew guava would bring the perfect acidity to a pre-dessert, and combining it with liquid cheesecake, which always makes me happy, was a no-brainer.

½ recipe	Liquid Cheesecake (page 149)
1 recipe	Guava Sorbet (recipe follows)
1 recipe	Cream Cheese Skin (recipe follows)

1. Use the back of a spoon to schmear (see page 29) a quarter of the liquid cheesecake into each of 4 bowls.

2. Make a quenelle (see page 28) or scoop of sorbet, transfer it to a clean spoon, and gently lower it into the cream cheese skin, then remove it immediately—the cold temperature of the guava sorbet will set the gelatin in the cream cheese mixture and create a "skin" around the sorbet. Place the enrobed sorbet in the center of 1 of the schmeared bowls. Repeat to make quenelles for the remaining bowls. Serve immediately.

guava sorbet

MAKES ABOUT 425 G (1 PINT)

Fresh guava always tastes a little funny to me, but I love guava nectar, which is why we chose to use it here in place of making our own puree from scratch. Guava nectar is easily found in the Goya aisle of nearly any grocery store. .

Powdered gelatin can be substituted for the sheet gelatin: use ½ teaspoon. In a pinch, substitute 35 g (2 tablespoons) corn syrup for the glucose.

Instead of a whisk, use a hand blender to mix the sorbet base.

While making the sorbet base, taste it. Do you think it should be sweeter? Saltier? Add more glucose, lime juice, or salt if necessary to balance (see page 26)

1	gelatin sheet	
325 g	guava nectar	1¼ cups
100 g	glucose	¼ cup
0.25 g	lime juice	⅛ teaspoon
1 g	kosher salt	¼ teaspoon

1. Bloom the gelatin (see page 29).

2. Warm a little bit of the guava nectar and whisk in the gelatin to dissolve. Whisk in the remaining guava nectar, the glucose, lime juice, and salt until everything is fully dissolved and incorporated.

3. Pour the mixture into your ice cream machine and freeze according to the manufacturer's instructions. The sorbet is best spun just before serving or using, but it will keep in an airtight container in the freezer for up to 2 weeks.

cream cheese skin

MAKES ABOUT 150 G (¾ CUP)

This recipe is simple yet magical. It will make you look like you paid $30,000 for a fancy culinary education when you dip the guava sorbet in it. It must be made right before you are going to use it, or it will set hard in your fridge, and trying to melt it back down and get it back to the perfect temperature will be the bane of your existence—the *opposite* of setting yourself up for success.

3	gelatin sheets		
55 g	cream cheese	2 ounces	
55 g	milk	¼ cup	
55 g	heavy cream	¼ cup	
25 g	glucose	1 tablespoon	
0.5 g	kosher salt	⅛ teaspoon	

Powdered gelatin can be substituted for the sheet gelatin: use 1½ teaspoons. In a pinch, substitute 9 g (2 teaspoons) corn syrup for the glucose.

Instead of a whisk, use a hand blender to mix the cream cheese skin.

1. Bloom the gelatin (see page 29).

2. Gently warm the cream cheese and milk in a small saucepan over low heat. When the mixture is very warm to the touch and just beginning to steam, remove it from heat, whisk in the bloomed gelatin, and watch it dissolve fully. Then whisk in the heavy cream, glucose, and salt.

3. Pour the contents of the pan into a deep round container (a plastic pint container works best) and leave it out on the counter while you gather your other elements to plate the dessert.

nut brittle

You'd think because I'm from the kind-of South, I'd have kind of grown up with brittle, peanut brittle at the very least. But no. My only exposure to it was at the occasional vacation spot, where it was often featured . . . with a side of fudge. But with texture being high on my list of must-haves for any creation that comes out of our kitchen, it was only a matter of time before I became obsessed with nut—and seed—brittles.

I have a serious ongoing affair with Heath bars and Skor bars for their English-style toffee bits and bites. The brittle became the closest, most reasonable thing to make and achieve a similar sweetness and crunch, without sticking butter into *everything* we make.

I rarely eat a big hunk of brittle. Instead, I love breaking it into much smaller pieces and then folding it into something tasty that needs more crunch or mixing it into a dough or batter for a heightened sense of surprise! texture. When baked into cookies or brownies, nut brittle melts into the butter of the recipe and takes on a butter toffee–style flavor and chomp (I swoon).

If I have time, I like to grind brittle down into a praline (it will liquefy with its own fats and a splash of oil) and eat it with a spoon or spread it on a cookie or on a piece of toast with a dusting of salt. It's the perfect sweet, nutty, salty snack that still holds splinters of flaky texture.

I'm not alone in this in the Momoverse. You can find nut brittles on the savory side of the Momofuku kitchen too. Oftentimes the savory cooks use glucose and Isomalt, a sugar substitute made from sugar beets, in place of some of the granulated sugar when making a caramel. These two sugars are less sweet than regular old granulated, making for a more savory brittle. Glucose and Isomalt also have properties that result in a less-brittle brittle—in other words, an easier-to-break brittle. The brittles in the savory kitchen also have salt and butter added to the caramel mix. These less sweet, less hard, rich nut brittles serve as a garnish in cold salads at Noodle Bar or as an unexpected textural element in the famous shaved foie gras at Ko. They balance the savory and acidic elements of their dishes and add crunch and just a hint of not-too-sweet sweetness.

peanut brittle

MAKES ABOUT 250 G (1¾ CUPS)

All of our nut brittles are extraordinarily simple. We use skinned (blanched) nuts, unroasted and unsalted. They take one part nuts to two parts sugar and about ten minutes of time. Nut brittles are one of few things we measure by volume, so no gram weights are needed here.

There will always be a small amount of caramel and nut left in the bottom of your pan after making the brittle. No worries! We've never met a person who can make this brittle without leaving a trace of it behind. Here's a hint: the best way to clean hardened caramel out of a pan is by putting water in it and boiling it. The hot water will dissolve the caramel and the pan will be a snap to clean.

1 cup	sugar
½ cup	peanuts

1. Line a quarter sheet pan with a Silpat (parchment will *not* work here).

2. Make a dry caramel: Heat the sugar in a small heavy-bottomed saucepan over medium-high heat. As soon as the sugar starts to melt, use a heatproof spatula to move it constantly around the pan—you want it all to melt and caramelize evenly. Cook and stir, cook and stir, until the caramel is a deep, dark amber, 3 to 5 minutes.

3. Once the caramel has reached the target color, remove the pan from the heat and, with the heatproof spatula, stir in the nuts. Make sure the nuts are coated in caramel, then dump the contents of the pan out onto the prepared sheet pan. Spread out as thin and evenly as possible. The caramel will set into a hard-to-move-around brittle mass in less than a minute, so work quickly. Let the brittle cool completely.

4. In a zip-top bag break the brittle up into pieces as small as possible with a meat pounder or a heavy rolling pin—we grind our brittle down in the food processor to the size of short-grain rice (you don't want anyone to chip a tooth on it!). Eat or cook with it at will. Store your brittle in an airtight container, and try to use it up within a month.

Elsewhere in this book: Peanut brittle is used in Peanut Butter Crunch (page 185).

hazelnut brittle

MAKES ABOUT 250 G (1¾ CUPS)

Follow the recipe for peanut brittle, substituting hazelnuts for the peanuts.

cashew brittle

MAKES ABOUT 375 G (2¼ CUPS)

Follow the recipe for peanut brittle, substituting ¾ cup cashews for the peanuts and increasing the sugar to 1½ cups.

pumpkin seed brittle

MAKES ABOUT 250 G (1¾ CUPS)

This, obviously, is made from a seed, not a nut, but it works just the same. We use pepitas, or hulled pumpkin seeds. We've tried making them from raw shelled seeds scooped straight from a pumpkin, but to no avail.

Follow the recipe for peanut brittle, substituting pumpkin seeds for the peanuts. When adding the seeds to the hot caramel, take care, they will "pop" a bit!

peanut butter cookies

MAKES 15 TO 20 COOKIES

This cookie dough is much softer than that of all the other cookie recipes in this book. Fear not: although there is a different ratio of butter to peanut butter to glucose, because peanut butter behaves differently than regular butter in baking recipes, this will yield the same crunchy-on-the-outside, fudgy-in-the-center Milk Bar cookie, I promise.

Make sure your brittle is ground down to the size of short-grain rice or the consistency and texture of your cookie will be off.

In a pinch, substitute 35 g (2 tablespoons) corn syrup for the glucose.

170 g	butter, at room temperature	12 tablespoons (1½ sticks)
300 g	sugar	1½ cups
100 g	glucose	¼ cup
260 g	Skippy peanut butter	1 cup
2	eggs	
0.5 g	vanilla extract	⅛ teaspoon
225 g	flour	1⅓ cups
2 g	baking powder	½ teaspoon
1 g	baking soda	⅛ teaspoon
9 g	kosher salt	2¼ teaspoons
½ recipe	Peanut Brittle (page 169)	

1. Combine the butter, sugar, and glucose in the bowl of a stand mixer fitted with the paddle attachment and cream together on medium-high for 2 to 3 minutes. Scrape down the sides of the bowl. Paddle in the peanut butter, then add the eggs and vanilla and beat for 30 seconds on medium-high speed. Scrape down the sides of the bowl, then beat on medium-high speed for 3 minutes. During this time the sugar granules will dissolve and the creamed mixture will double in size. (The lower proportion of butter and the presence of peanut butter—which is a great emulsifier—means you don't need to do the standard 10-minute creaming for this cookie.)

2. Reduce the mixer speed to low and add the flour, baking powder, baking soda, and salt. Mix just until the dough comes together, no longer than 1 minute. (Do not walk away from the machine during this step, or you will risk overmixing the dough.) Scrape down the sides of the bowl.

3. Still on low speed, mix in the peanut brittle until incorporated, no more than 30 seconds.

4. Using a 2¾-ounce ice cream scoop (or a ⅓-cup measure), portion out the dough onto a parchment-lined sheet pan. Pat the tops of the cookie dough domes flat. Wrap the sheet pan tightly in plastic wrap and refrigerate for at least 1 hour, or for up to 1 week. Do *not* bake your cookies from room temperature—they will not bake properly.

5. Heat the oven to 375°F.

6. Arrange the chilled dough a minimum of 4 inches apart on parchment- or Silpat-lined sheet pans. Bake for 18 minutes. The cookies will puff, crackle, and spread. After 18 minutes, they should be tan with auburn specks throughout. Give them an extra minute or so if that's not the case.

7. Cool the cookies completely on the sheet pans before transferring to a plate or an airtight container for storage. At room temp, cookies will keep fresh for 5 days; in the freezer, they will keep for 1 month.

candy bar pie

MAKES 1 (10-INCH) PIE; SERVES 8

During many a week, candy bars make up 50 percent (or more) of my diet. As a teen, I already showed a predilection for staying hip to the culinary scene at the grocery store, trolling the aisles to check out interesting frozen items, new cereals, perhaps a vamped-up cookie section, and, of course, the impulse-buy area—one of my favorites—with its multitude of candy bars trying to break into the market.

Which is why I was hooked on Take 5 candy bars long before I ever thought about making a pie inspired by them. I was blown away by my first bite of one, in the passenger seat of the family van in the Giant parking lot of NoVa. My sister had one cluster, and the other was all mine. It is the epitome of perfectly layered chocolate, peanuts, caramel, peanut butter, and pretzels. Hershey's describes it as "a unique taste experience combining five favorite ingredients in one candy bar. The result is a delicious salty sweet snack unlike anything else." Amazing.

For my birthday a couple of years ago, Dave bought me two cases, that's 480 clusters, of Take 5 candy bars and dared me to eat them all in a month. With a little help from my friends, I did it in twenty-eight days. On my birthday, that first day, I ate seven—and then puked the next morning (bad idea).

Marian Mar made a big push to get this pie on the opening menu of Milk Bar, because, as she once put it, we *are* candy bars, and candy bars *are* us. So we *need* a candy bar pie on the menu. It's a little bit of a bitch to make, which was my main argument for wanting to leave it off the menu. But working in this industry is a labor of love, after all, and Marian was right all along. This pie is one of our top sellers even today. We lovingly refer to it at Milk Bar as the T-5 pie.

In this recipe, we make a chocolate glaze for the top of the pie using dark chocolate, white chocolate, and oil. I like to refer to it as "cleverly avoiding tempering chocolate," which is a fussy, somewhat temperamental way of structuring chocolate so that it sets with a shiny, crisp coat. But stirring oil into melted chocolate allows us to glaze the top of the pie with a brush and set it in the refrigerator. The chocolate still has a nice, thin crispness while maintaining a certain malleability, ensuring a clean cut down through the many layers of the pie.

Toasting pretzels deepens their flavor significantly.

Note that the nougat must be made within 5 or 10 minutes of when you want to press it into the pie.

1 recipe	Salty Caramel (recipe follows), melted		
1 recipe	Chocolate Crust (page 92), refrigerated		
8	mini pretzels		
1 recipe	Peanut Butter Nougat (recipe follows)		
45 g	55% chocolate	1½ ounces
45 g	white chocolate	1½ ounces
20 g	grapeseed oil	2 tablespoons

recipe continues

1. Pour the salty caramel into the crust. Return it to the fridge to set for at least 4 hours, or overnight.

2. Heat the oven to 300°F.

3. Spread the pretzels out on a sheet pan and toast for 20 minutes, or until they have slightly darkened in color and the kitchen smells pretzely. Set aside to cool.

4. Fetch the pie from the fridge and cover the face of the hardened caramel with the nougat. Use the palms of your hands to press down and smooth the nougat into an even layer. Return the pie to the fridge and let the nougat firm up for 1 hour.

5. Make a chocolate glaze by combining the chocolates and the oil in a microwave-safe bowl and gently melting them on medium in 30-second increments, stirring between blasts. Once the chocolate is melted, whisk the mixture until smooth and shiny. Use the glaze the same day, or store in an airtight container at room temperature for up to 3 weeks.

6. Finish that pie: Remove it from the refrigerator and, using a pastry brush, paint a thin layer of the chocolate glaze over the nougat, covering it completely. (If the glaze has firmed up, gently warm it so it is easy to paint on the pie.) Arrange the pretzels evenly around the edges of the pie. Use the pastry brush to paint the remaining chocolate glaze in a thin layer over the pretzels, sealing their freshness and flavor.

7. Put the pie in the fridge for at least 15 minutes to set the chocolate. Wrapped in plastic, the pie will keep fresh in the fridge for 3 weeks or in the freezer for up to 2 months; defrost before serving.

8. Cut the pie into 8 slices, using the pretzels as your guide: each slice should have a whole pretzel on it.

salty caramel

MAKES ABOUT 320 G (1½ CUPS)

105 g	heavy cream	½ cup
25 g	butter	2 tablespoons
4 g	vanilla extract	1 teaspoon
4 g	kosher salt	1 teaspoon
130 g	sugar	⅔ cup
100 g	glucose	¼ cup
1	gelatin sheet	
105 g	heavy cream	½ cup

1. Put 105 g (½ cup) heavy cream, butter, vanilla, and salt in a medium bowl and set aside.

2. Make a caramel: Heat the sugar and glucose in a medium heavy-bottomed saucepan over medium-high heat. As soon as the sugar starts to melt, use a heatproof spatula to move it constantly around the pan—you want it all to melt and caramelize evenly. Cook and stir, cook and stir, until the caramel is a deep, dark amber, 3 to 5 minutes.

3. Meanwhile, bloom the gelatin (see page 29).

4. Once the caramel has reached the target color, remove the saucepan from the heat. Very slowly and very carefully pour the remaining 105 g (½ cup) heavy cream into the caramel. The caramel will bubble up and steam; stand away until the steam dissipates. Whisk the mixture together. If it is at all lumpy, or there are any clumps of hardened caramel floating around the cream, put the saucepan back over medium heat and heat the mixture, whisking constantly, until all of the caramel has dissolved and the mixture is smooth; remove the pan from the heat.

5. Whisk the bloomed gelatin into the caramel. Once all of the gelatin has dissolved, pour the caramel through a fine-mesh sieve into the bowl with the butter. Let the mixture sit, undisturbed, for 2 minutes, then begin whisking. Whisk slowly at first to prevent the hot cream from splashing up and burning you, then continue whisking until the mixture is completely homogenous.

6. Use immediately, or store in an airtight container in the fridge for up to 3 weeks. When ready to use, simply melt it in the microwave in 30-second increments, stirring between blasts until it is completely liquid.

Powdered gelatin can be substituted for the sheet gelatin: use ½ teaspoon. In a pinch, substitute 35 g (2 tablespoons) corn syrup for the glucose.

Instead of a whisk, use a hand blender to mix the caramel base.

recipe continues

peanut butter nougat

MAKES ABOUT 250 G (1 CUP), OR ENOUGH FOR 1 CANDY BAR PIE OR PB & J PIE

This recipe involves heating two separate amounts of sugar, each one to a different temperature. Why do we do it that way? Because that's the correct way to make a nougat. If there were a way around it, I'm pretty sure we would have found it by now and dear diaried you about it in the technique portion of this lovely book. We use peanut butter nougat in several of our pies, the most popular being the candy bar pie.

If you feel a snack attack coming on and peanuts are not your jam, substitute hazelnut paste for peanut butter and hazelnut brittle for the peanut brittle.

25 g	sugar	2 tablespoons
20 g	water	1½ tablespoons
40 g	sugar	3 tablespoons
20 g	water	1½ tablespoons
1	egg white	
65 g	Skippy peanut butter	¼ cup
½ recipe	Peanut Brittle (page 169)	
2 g	kosher salt	½ teaspoon

1. Put the first measures of sugar and water in a tiny saucepan and gently slush the sugar around in the water until it feels like wet sand. Do the same thing with the second measures of sugar and water in another tiny saucepan.

2. Place both saucepans on the stove and begin heating them up: turn the heat up to medium under the first sugar measurement and keep the heat low under the second measurement. Heat the first sugar up to 115°C (239°F), keeping track of the temperature with an instant-read or candy thermometer.

3. While the sugar is heating up, put the egg white in the bowl of a stand mixer and, with the whisk attachment, begin whipping it to medium-soft peaks. If the white reaches medium-soft peaks before the first sugar hits 115°C (239°F), slow your mixer *way* down and let the sugar catch up. Or, if you notice that the sugar is almost to 115°C (239°F) and the white is still a bit off, turn the heat *way* down under the sugar and turn the speed way up on the mixer. Ideally, the white will reach medium-soft peaks at exactly the same time as the first sugar measurement hits its mark. If you can achieve this on your first try, then we have a job waiting for you in our kitchen.

4. Once the first sugar measurement reaches 115°C (239°F), remove it from the heat and very carefully pour it into the whipping egg white, being careful to avoid the whisk: turn the mixer down to a very low speed before you do this, unless you want some interesting burn marks on your face. Once all of the sugar is successfully added to the egg white, turn the mixer speed back up, and turn the heat way up under the second sugar measurement. Once this sugar reaches 120°C (248°F), remove it from the heat and pour it into the whipping egg white, taking the same precautions as with the first sugar measurement. Let the egg white whip until cool.

5. While the white is whipping, mix the peanut butter, peanut brittle, and salt in a large bowl until well blended.

6. Once the white has cooled to room temperature, turn the mixer off, remove the bowl, and, using a spatula, fold the white into the peanut butter mixture. Use immediately in the candy bar pie assembly. Once it cools, the nougat is only acceptable as a ridiculously delicious snack, sure to steal any peanut butter lover's heart.

Elsewhere in this book: The nougat is also used in the PB & J pie (page 63).

blondie pie

MAKES 1 (10-INCH) PIE; SERVES 8 TO 10

If nut brittle is my muse, blondie pie is our love child. It is, to date, my favorite pie we've ever created. Dense, sweet, salty, nutty, chock-full of textures large and small, it's perfect to grab a piece of on the go and crush as if it were a slice of pizza.

¾ recipe	Graham Crust (page 112)	255 g (1½ cups)
1 recipe	Blondie Pie Filling (recipe follows)	
1 recipe	Cashew Praline (recipe follows)	

1. Heat the oven to 325°F.

2. Dump the graham crust into a 10-inch pie tin. With your fingers and the palms of your hands, press the crust firmly into the pie tin, covering the bottom and sides evenly. Set aside while you make the filling. Wrapped in plastic, the crust can be refrigerated or frozen for up to 2 weeks.

3. Put the pie tin on a sheet pan and pour in the blondie pie filling. Bake the pie for 30 minutes. It will set slightly in the center and darken in color. Add 3 to 5 minutes if that's not the case. Let cool to room temperature.

4. Just before serving, cover the top of the pie with the cashew praline.

Any other nut (brittle and praline) will do in this pie, but cashews balance the white chocolate so well without overwhelming the other ingredients. With a stronger nut, this will most likely become a peanut butter blondie pie, or a hazelnut blondie pie, etc.

Warm the graham crust slightly in the microwave to make it easy to mold.

blondie pie filling

MAKES ABOUT 540 G (2¼ CUPS)

160 g	white chocolate	5½ ounces	
55 g	butter	4 tablespoons (½ stick)	
2	egg yolks		
40 g	sugar	3 tablespoons	
105 g	heavy cream	½ cup	
52 g	flour	⅓ cup	
½ recipe	Cashew Brittle (page 170)		
4 g	kosher salt	1 teaspoon	

Elsewhere in this book: Blondie pie is great as a fall pie when garnished with Pumpkin Ganache (page 208).

1. Combine the white chocolate and butter in a microwave-safe bowl and gently melt them on medium, in 30-second increments, stirring between blasts. Once melted, whisk the mixture until smooth.

2. Put the egg yolks and sugar in a medium bowl and whisk together until smooth. Pour in the white chocolate mixture and whisk to combine. Slowly drizzle in the heavy cream and whisk to combine.

3. Stir the flour, cashew brittle, and salt together in a small bowl, then carefully fold them into the filling. Use immediately, or store in an airtight container in the fridge for up to 2 weeks.

cashew praline

MAKES ABOUT 180 G (½ CUP)

½ recipe	Cashew Brittle (page 170)	
20 g	grapeseed oil	2 tablespoons

Grind the brittle with the oil in a food processor until it has completely broken down and almost liquefied. Boom: it's praline. Look at how easy that was. Store in an airtight container in the fridge for up to 1 month or in the freezer for up to 2 months.

hazelnut praline

MAKES ABOUT 120 G (½ CUP)

Mix hazelnut praline with Fudge Sauce (page 136) for your own makeshift Nutella with little bits of texture in every bite.

Follow the recipe for cashew praline, substituting hazelnut brittle for the cashew brittle.

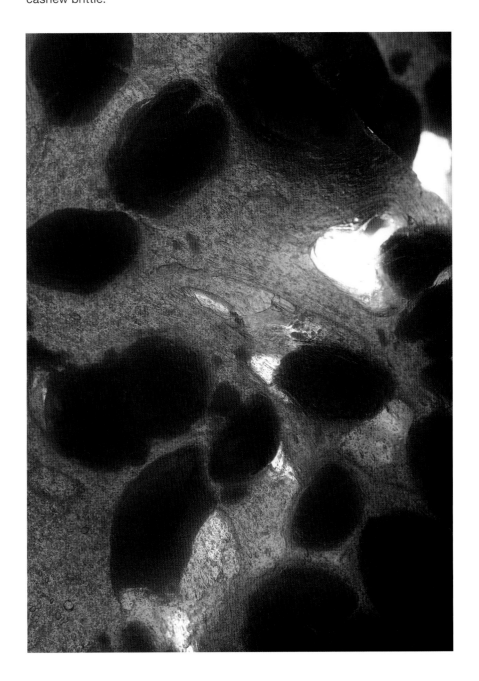

nut crunch

The origin of the nut crunch in our kitchen is a funny one. It was more like the invasion of the feuilletine in the basement of Ssäm Bar. At the time, I had two desserts on the menu at Ssäm Bar and a small soft-serve program going at Noodle Bar. I knew I'd have to step it up for Ko's opening, and I still wasn't too steady on my identity as a pastry person who created things. I figured I'd start by filling the pastry shelf with more than just eggs, flour, salt, sugar, milk powder, and chocolate.

So I turned to old notebooks from restaurants where I had worked in the past. Any good cook keeps a notebook of recipes, thoughts, ideas, prep lists, and so on. I flipped through the pages to remember what ingredients pastry chefs of my past liked to use. Nuts! That's right! Nut pastes! Nut flours! Nut oils! All good pastry chefs use one or more of those for flavor, texture, and nuance—and because they're available year-round. Vanilla beans, pass. Rose water, pass. Coconut flakes, meh. Cocoa nibs, maybe. Feuilletine! That's right. I'd mixed feuilletine, hazelnut paste, and chocolate to make a bar of crunchy crust for a parfait. And I'd tossed feuilletine in hazelnut paste and white chocolate to make clusters of candy for a parting gift to present to a table with the check.

I put on blinders while looking through my old recipes, searching only for ones that used feuilletine. I springboarded into a brainstorm of possibilities. What if I changed the nut paste flavor? Used a higher ratio of nut paste or a higher ratio of feuilletine? Tossed in some nuts to really showcase the nut itself—or, better yet, some nut brittle for an off-the-charts texture? The "nut crunch" came to life.

Not to be confused with "the crunch" (page 49), "nut crunch" is a crunch based on a nut paste, seasoned with confectioners' sugar (because it dissolves quickly in the mixing process) and salt. We fold in lightly toasted nuts or nut brittles for depth and texture, in addition to the feuilletine, of course, which started it all.

peanut butter crunch

MAKES ABOUT 515 G (3½ CUPS)

195 g	Skippy peanut butter	¾ cup
⅓ recipe	Peanut Brittle (page 169)	80 g (½ cup)
120 g	feuilletine	1½ cups
120 g	confectioners' sugar	¾ cup
2 g	kosher salt	½ teaspoon

If you want to make this nut crunch gluten-free, substitute ½ recipe peanut brittle for the feuilletine.

Combine the peanut butter, brittle, feuilletine, confectioners' sugar, and salt in the bowl of a stand mixer fitted with the paddle attachment and paddle on medium-low speed for about 1 minute, until homogenous. The crunch can be stored in an airtight container at room temperature for 5 days or in the fridge for up to 2 weeks.

hazelnut crunch

MAKES ABOUT 280 G (2 CUPS)

100 g	hazelnut paste	⅓ cup
⅓ recipe	Hazelnut Brittle (page 170)	80 g (½ cup)
80 g	feuilletine	1 cup
20 g	confectioners' sugar	2 tablespoons
3 g	kosher salt	¾ teaspoon

If you want to make this nut crunch gluten-free, substitute ½ recipe hazelnut brittle for the feuilletine.

Follow the procedure for the peanut butter crunch, substituting the hazelnut paste and brittle for the peanut butter and brittle.

pistachio crunch

MAKES ABOUT 330 G (2 CUPS)

75 g	pistachios, raw, unsalted	½ cup

155 g	pistachio paste	½ cup
60 g	feuilletine	¾ cup
40 g	confectioners' sugar	¼ cup
4 g	kosher salt	1 teaspoon

If you want to make this nut crunch gluten-free, substitute 75 g (½ cup) additional toasted ground pistachios for the feuilletine; used as the replacement for the milk crumbs, this makes the amazing almond flour Pistachio Layer Cake (page 83) entirely gluten-free.

Elsewhere in this book: Pistachio crunch is used in the Chèvre Frozen Yogurt dessert (page 217).

1. Heat the oven to 325°F.

2. Put the pistachios on a sheet pan and toast in the oven for 15 minutes. Cool to room temperature.

3. Put the toasted pistachios in a clean kitchen towel and, with a sauté pan or a rolling pin, bash them into smaller pieces, ideally halving the pistachios, or breaking them down to no smaller than one-eighth their original size.

4. Combine the broken pistachios with the pistachio paste, feuilletine, confectioners' sugar, and salt in the bowl of a stand mixer fitted with the paddle attachment and paddle on medium-low speed for about 1 minute, until homogenous. The crunch can be stored in an airtight container at room temperature for 5 days or in the fridge for up to 2 weeks.

thai tea crunch

MAKES ABOUT 140 G (1 CUP)

15 g	slivered almonds	2 tablespoons
55 g	almond butter	¼ cup
40 g	feuilletine	½ cup
30 g	confectioners' sugar	3 tablespoons
2 g	kosher salt	½ teaspoon
8 g	Thai black tea leaves	1½ tablespoons
0.25 g	citric acid (see page 16)	scant pinch

Follow the procedure for the pistachio nut crunch, substituting the almonds for the pistachios and the almond butter for the pistachio paste, adding the tea leaves and citric acid with the dry ingredients.

Omit the tea leaves for an "almond crunch" to use in your own dessert concoction.

pb & j
saltine panna cotta, concord grape jelly, peanut butter crunch

SERVES 4

In the fall of 2008, Ssäm Bar needed a seasonal dessert, and Concord grapes were on the brain. Best man I know suggested I do a take on a pb & j, but my way, using techniques and perhaps a flavor that made sense but was unexpected. I chose the path of a panna cotta, made with milk steeped with the flavor of a saltine cracker: salty and soda-y—a poor man's pb & j. People were going to love it or hate it. And that was perfectly fine with me, because I loved it, though the saltine milk is not for wussies.

½ recipe	Concord Grape Jelly (recipe follows)
½ recipe	Peanut Butter Crunch (page 185)
1 recipe	Saltine Panna Cotta (recipe follows)

For an upscale option, garnish the panna cottas with any leftover saltine crackers. We crumble a small amount between thumb and index finger just before serving.

1. Divide the jelly evenly among 4 serving bowls.

2. Put a 1-inch circular cookie cutter or ring mold on a small plate and use a spoon to firmly press one-quarter of the peanut butter crunch into the circle, making a ½-inch-high round. Transfer the round of crunch to the first bowl, popping it out of the mold onto the jelly. Repeat for the remaining 3 bowls.

3. With an offset spatula, carefully transfer 1 panna cotta to the top of each peanut butter crunch round. Serve immediately.

concord grape jelly

MAKES ABOUT 315 G (1¼ CUPS)

50 g	sugar	¼ cup
3 g	pectin NH (see page 20)	1½ teaspoons
0.5 g	kosher salt	⅛ teaspoon

½ recipe	Concord Grape Juice (page 64)	

1. Whisk together the sugar, pectin, and salt in a medium pot or saucepan. Slowly whisk in the grape juice and bring to a full, rolling boil. Reduce the heat and cook at a low boil for 2 minutes to activate the pectin and turn the juice into a beautiful jelly. Your kitchen will begin to smell like grape-flavored bubble gum. This is a good sign.

2. Once the pectin has been activated and coats the back of a spoon, remove the jelly from the heat. The jelly can be stored in an airtight container in the fridge for up to 2 weeks.

saltine panna cotta

SERVES 4

55 g	saltine crackers	½ sleeve
220 g	milk	1 cup
160 g	heavy cream	¾ cup
150 g	sugar	¾ cup
12 g	kosher salt	1 tablespoon
6 g	baking soda	1 teaspoon
1½	gelatin sheets	
	Pam or other nonstick cooking spray	

Toasting the saltines deepens the flavor of the steeped milk.

Powdered gelatin can be substituted for the sheet gelatin: use ¾ teaspoon.

1. Heat the oven to 250°F.

2. Put the saltines on a parchment-lined sheet pan. Bake for 20 minutes to toast them lightly. Cool completely.

3. Transfer the saltines to a blender, pour in the milk, and blend on high for about 20 seconds. Immediately strain the saltine milk through a fine-mesh sieve into a medium bowl, using your hand or the back of a ladle to wring all the milk out of the saltines. Do not force any mushy saltines through the sieve. (We compost the mush.)

4. Whisk in the heavy cream, sugar, salt, and baking soda until fully dissolved.

5. Bloom the gelatin (see page 29).

6. Pour the saltine mixture into a medium saucepan and heat until warm to the touch. Remove from the heat, add the bloomed gelatin, and whisk until dissolved.

7. Lightly Pam-spray 4 (2-ounce) circular molds. We use silicone molds for ease of removal once the panna cottas are set. Put the molds on a flat, transportable surface. Pour the saltine panna cotta base into the molds and transfer to the freezer to set for at least 3 hours, or overnight.

8. Remove the panna cottas from their molds by gently popping them out or by plunging the bases of the molds into warm water for 3 seconds, then tapping them upside down on the counter. Stored in an airtight container, the panna cottas will keep in the freezer for 1 month. Thaw before serving, either overnight in the fridge or for 3 hours at room temperature.

banana layer cake

MAKES 1 (6-INCH) LAYER CAKE, 5 TO 6 INCHES TALL; SERVES 6 TO 8

Like the candy bar pie, this banana cake is a doozy to make, but it's here because it's a bestseller at Milk Bar—so much so, that in two years, it is the *only* cake that has never been rotated out, based on season or popularity. It is Oprah's favorite cake, and it will be yours too.

1 recipe	Banana Cake (recipe follows)	
55 g	milk	¼ cup
1 recipe	Chocolate Hazelnut Ganache (recipe follows), warmed	
½ recipe	Hazelnut Crunch (page 185)	
½ recipe	Banana Cream (page 91)	
1 recipe	Hazelnut Frosting (recipe follows)	

special equipment

1 (6-inch) cake ring

2 strips acetate, each 3 inches wide and 20 inches long

Save a perfectly ripe banana or leftover hazelnut brittle to garnish this cake in addition to the hazelnut crunch clusters.

1. Put a piece of parchment or a Silpat on the counter. Invert the cake onto it and peel off the parchment or Silpat from the bottom of the cake. Use the cake ring to stamp out 2 circles from the cake. These are your top 2 cake layers. The remaining cake "scrap" will come together to make the bottom layer of the cake.

layer 1, the bottom
2. Clean the cake ring and place it in the center of a sheet pan lined with clean parchment or a Silpat. Use 1 strip of acetate to line the inside of the cake ring.

3. Put the cake scraps inside the ring and use the back of your hand to tamp the cake scraps together into a flat even layer.

4. Dunk a pastry brush in the milk and give the layer of cake a good, healthy bath of half of the milk.

recipe continues

5. Use the back of a spoon to spread half of the ganache in an even layer over the cake.

6. Sprinkle one-third of the hazelnut crunch evenly over the ganache. Use the back of your hand to anchor it in place.

7. Use the back of a spoon to spread half of the banana cream as evenly as possible over the crunch.

layer 2, the middle
8. With your index finger, gently tuck the second strip of acetate between the cake ring and the top ¼ inch of the first strip of acetate, so that you have a clear ring of acetate 5 to 6 inches tall—high enough to support the height of the finished cake. Set a cake round on top of the banana cream and repeat the process for layer 1 (if 1 of your 2 cake rounds is jankier than the other, use it here in the middle and save the prettier one for the top).

layer 3, the top
9. Nestle the remaining cake round into the banana cream. Cover the top of the cake with all the hazelnut frosting. Give it volume and swirls, or do as we do and opt for a perfectly flat top. Garnish the frosting with the remaining clusters of hazelnut crunch.

10. Transfer the sheet pan to the freezer and freeze for a minimum of 12 hours to set the cake and filling. The cake will keep in the freezer for up to 2 weeks.

11. At least 3 hours before you are ready to serve the cake, pull the sheet pan out of the freezer and, using your fingers and thumbs, pop the cake out of the cake ring. Gently peel off the acetate and transfer the cake to a platter or cake stand. Let it defrost in the fridge for a minimum of 3 hours (wrapped well in plastic, the cake can be refrigerated for up to 5 days).

12. Slice the cake into wedges and serve.

banana cake

MAKES 1 QUARTER SHEET PAN

You wouldn't believe how hard it is to make a good banana cake. I'm talking about a sheet cake that tastes like banana bread, but not too dry, not too tough, and not dense and fudgy, like the dead center of banana bread can be at times. For weeks, maybe even a month, we worked on a banana cake in the basement of Ko. It felt like a lifetime—and still we weren't getting anywhere close. That is, until Emily, our extern, came in with her mother's sacred banana cake recipe. We adapted it, but this recipe belongs to the heart of her family. Mrs. Kritemeyer, we love you!

85 g	butter, at room temperature	6 tablespoons
200 g	sugar	1 cup
1	egg	
110 g	buttermilk	½ cup
20 g	grapeseed oil	2 tablespoons
2 g	banana extract	½ teaspoon
225 g	*rrrrrripe* bananas	2
225 g	flour	1⅓ cups
3 g	baking powder	¾ teaspoon
3 g	baking soda	½ teaspoon
2 g	kosher salt	½ teaspoon
	Pam or other nonstick cooking spray (optional)	

Just as with the Banana Cream (page 91), the riper and browner the banana, the tastier the cake.

1. Heat the oven to 325°F.

2. Combine the butter and sugar in the bowl of a stand mixer fitted with the paddle attachment and cream together on medium-high for 2 to 3 minutes. Scrape down the sides of the bowl, add the egg, and mix on medium-high again for 2 to 3 minutes. Scrape down the sides of the bowl once more.

3. Stream in the buttermilk, oil, and banana extract while the paddle swirls on low speed. Increase the mixer speed to medium-high and paddle for 5 to 6 minutes, until the mixture is practically white, twice the size of your original fluffy butter-and-sugar mixture, and completely homogenous. You're basically forcing too much liquid into an already fatty mixture that doesn't want to make

recipe continues

room for it, so if it doesn't look right after 6 minutes, keep mixing. Stop the mixer and scrape down the sides of the bowl.

4. On very low speed, add the bananas and mix for 45 to 60 seconds to ensure all the bananas are broken apart.

5. Still on low speed, add the flour, baking powder, baking soda, and salt and mix for 45 to 60 seconds, just until your batter comes together and any remnants of dry ingredients have been incorporated. Scrape down the sides of the bowl.

6. Pam-spray a quarter sheet pan and line with parchment, or just line the pan with a Silpat. Using a spatula, spread the cake batter in an even layer in the pan. Give the bottom of your sheet pan a tap on the countertop to even out the layer (this cake batter is very forgiving). Bake for 25 to 30 minutes. The cake will rise and puff, doubling in size, but will remain slightly buttery and dense. At 25 minutes, gently poke the edge of the cake with your finger: the cake should bounce back slightly and the center should no longer be jiggly. Leave the cake in the oven for an extra 3 to 5 minutes if the cake doesn't pass these tests.

7. Take the cake out of the oven and cool on a wire rack or, in a pinch, in the fridge or freezer (don't worry, it's not cheating). The cooled cake can be stored in the fridge, wrapped in plastic wrap, for up to 5 days.

chocolate hazelnut ganache

MAKES ABOUT 215 G (⅔ CUP)

55 g	heavy cream	¼ cup
60 g	gianduja chocolate, melted	2 ounces
65 g	hazelnut paste	¼ cup
¼ recipe	Fudge Sauce (page 136)	38 g (3 tablespoons)
1 g	kosher salt	¼ teaspoon

1. Bring the heavy cream to a boil in a small heavy-bottomed saucepan over medium-high heat.

2. Meanwhile, combine the melted gianduja, hazelnut paste, fudge sauce, and salt in a medium bowl.

3. Pour the cream into the bowl and let sit undisturbed for 1 minute. With a hand blender or a whisk, slowly mix the contents of the bowl until the mixture is glossy and silky-smooth. This will take 2 to 4 minutes, depending on your speed and strength. Use immediately, or store in an airtight container in the fridge for up to 2 weeks; do not freeze.

hazelnut frosting

MAKES ABOUT 110 G (⅓ CUP)

25 g	butter, at room temperature	2 tablespoons
65 g	hazelnut paste	¼ cup
20 g	confectioners' sugar	2 tablespoons
0.5 g	kosher salt	⅛ teaspoon

1. Put the butter in the bowl of a stand mixer fitted with the paddle attachment and paddle on medium-high speed until it is completely smooth. Scrape down the sides of the bowl with a spatula. This is a small amount of ingredients so use your granny mixer now or take on the task by hand in a medium bowl.

2. Add the hazelnut paste, confectioners' sugar, and salt and mix on high speed until the frosting is fluffy and has no lumps in it, 3 to 4 minutes. Scrape down the sides of the bowl and mix for 15 seconds, just to be sure everything is nice and smooth. Use immediately, or store in an airtight container in the fridge for up to 1 month. Bring to room temperature before using.

Gianduja is a sweet chocolate that contains hazelnut paste. It's like a soft brick of Nutella—pick it up at a specialty grocery store or online. We use Cacao Barry gianduja.

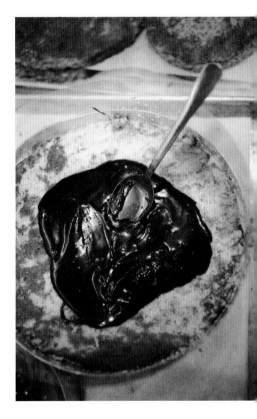

lemon meringue–pistachio pie

MAKES 1 (10-INCH) PIE; SERVES 8 TO 10

Nut crunch makes a great pie crust! I absolutely love this pie, but it doesn't fit into the composed dessert realm of Ssäm Bar's menu and it isn't quick and easy to pack like Milk Bar pies need to be, so it never made it onto a menu. It's a delicious recipe you'll only find here.

Painting a thin layer of white chocolate onto the pie crust protects it from getting soggy from the moisture in the lemon curd. This is a classic pastry trick when filling any crust with something that is moist or somewhat wet.

Note that you will need a full recipe of lemon curd here, but it's broken up in the ingredients list because two-thirds is used in one spot and the remaining third in another.

1 recipe	Pistachio Crunch (page 186)	
15 g	white chocolate, melted	½ ounce
⅔ recipe	Lemon Curd (page 86)	305 g (1⅓ cups)
200 g	sugar	1 cup
100 g	water	½ cup
3	egg whites	
⅓ recipe	Lemon Curd (page 86)	155 g (⅔ cup)

1. Dump the pistachio crunch into a 10-inch pie tin. With your fingers and the palms of your hands, press the crunch firmly into the pie tin, making sure the bottom and sides are evenly covered. Set aside while you make the filling; wrapped in plastic, the crust can be refrigerated, for up to 2 weeks.

2. Using a pastry brush, paint a thin layer of the white chocolate onto the bottom and up the sides of the crust. Put the crust in the freezer for 10 minutes to set the chocolate.

3. Put 305 g (1⅓ cups) lemon curd into a small bowl and stir to loosen it a bit. Scrape the lemon curd into a crust and use the back of a spoon or a spatula to spread it in an even layer. Place the pie in the freezer for about 10 minutes to help set the lemon curd layer.

4. Meanwhile, combine the sugar and water in a small heavy-bottomed saucepan and gently slush the sugar around in the water until it feels like wet sand. Place the saucepan over medium heat and heat the mixture up to 115°C (239°F), keeping track of the temperature with an instant-read or candy thermometer.

5. While the sugar is heating up, put the egg whites in the bowl of a stand mixer and, with the whisk attachment, begin whipping them to medium-soft peaks. If the whites reach medium-soft peaks before the sugar hits 115°C (239°F), slow your mixer waaaaaay down and let the sugar catch up. Or, if you notice that the sugar is almost to 115°C (239°F) and the whites are still a bit off, turn the heat *way* down under the sugar and turn the speed way up on the mixer. Ideally, the whites will reach medium-soft peaks at exactly the same time as the sugar syrup hits the 115°C (239°F) mark. If you can achieve this on your first try, then we have a job waiting for you in our kitchen.

6. Once the sugar syrup reaches 115°C (239°F), remove it from the heat and very carefully pour it into the whipping egg whites, being sure to avoid the whisk: turn the mixer down to very low speed before you do this, unless you want some interesting burn marks on your face. Once all of the sugar is successfully added to the egg whites, turn the mixer speed back up and let the meringue whip until it has cooled to room temperature.

7. While the meringue is whipping, put the 155 g (⅔ cup) lemon curd in a large bowl and stir, using a spatula, to loosen it up a bit.

8. When the meringue has cooled to room temperature, turn the mixer off, remove the bowl, and fold the meringue into the lemon curd with the spatula until no white streaks remain, being careful not to deflate the meringue.

9. Remove the pie from the freezer and scoop the lemon meringue on top of the lemon curd. Using a spoon, spread the meringue in an even layer, completely covering the lemon curd.

10. Serve, or store the pie in the freezer until ready to use. Wrapped tightly in plastic wrap once frozen hard, it will keep in the freezer for up to 3 weeks. Let the pie defrost overnight in the fridge or for at least 3 hours at room temperature before serving.

thai tea parfait
lemon mascarpone, thai tea crunch

SERVES 4

We made this dessert because of our love for Thai tea sweetened just the way the Thai do, with sweetened condensed milk. We got so many compliments on it that we left it on the Ssäm Bar dessert menu for over a year, which we almost never do. To this day, we still get requests for it. While the ingredients here are off the beaten path of your average pantry, they can easily be found in Chinatown or a Latin market or at amazon.com.

100 g	water	½ cup
10 g	Thai tea leaves	2 tablespoons
1	gelatin sheet	
75 g	sweetened condensed milk	¼ cup
16 g	store-bought dulce de leche	1 tablespoon
6 g	tamarind paste	1 teaspoon
1 g	kosher salt	¼ teaspoon
	Pam or other nonstick cooking spray	
75 g	heavy cream	⅓ cup
35 g	sour cream	2 tablespoons
1 recipe	Lemon Mascarpone (recipe follows)	
1 recipe	Thai Tea Crunch (page 187)	
4	mint sprigs	

Powdered gelatin can be substituted for the sheet gelatin: use ½ teaspoon.

1. Combine the water and tea leaves in a blender and blend on high for 10 seconds. Let the mixture steep for 30 minutes.

2. Strain the liquid through a fine sieve into a small bowl and reserve. (If there is any grit left in the tea steep, pass it through a coffee filter to remove it.)

3. Bloom the gelatin (see page 29).

recipe continues

4. Heat the Thai tea steep in a small saucepan until it is warm to the touch. Add the bloomed gelatin and stir until the gelatin is fully dissolved. Pour into a medium bowl and whisk in the condensed milk, dulce de leche, tamarind paste, and salt until all the ingredients are dissolved and fully incorporated.

5. Put the bowl in the fridge for about 20 minutes, whisking it every 5 minutes or so. Check the consistency of the base as you whisk it; you don't want the parfait to set fully, but you want it to get thick enough to be able to fold in the whipped heavy cream mixture and have it hold its shape a bit. The best description for the consistency you are looking for is that of a really thick porridge. Pretend you are Goldilocks and that you are waiting for it to be just right. Pigtails are optional.

6. While the base is setting, lightly Pam-spray 4 (2-ounce) molds of your choice. We use silicone molds for ease of removal after the parfaits have set. Put the molds on a flat, transportable surface; set aside.

7. Whisk the heavy cream and sour cream (in a mixer with the whisk attachment, or by hand) until the mixture reaches medium-soft peaks. If the heavy cream mixture is ready before the parfait base has set, put it in the fridge until ready to use.

8. Once the consistency of the parfait base has reached perfection, pour it into a large bowl and, using a spatula, fold in the heavy cream mixture until the mixture is completely smooth and no white streaks remain. Pour the parfait into the prepared molds, and carefully tap the molds on the countertop a few times to remove excess air bubbles. Freeze for at least 3 hours, or overnight.

9. Unmold the frozen parfaits by gently popping them out of their molds or by plunging the base of the molds into warm water for 3 seconds, then tapping them upside down on the counter. Stored in an airtight container, the parfaits will keep in the freezer for 1 month. Thaw before serving, either overnight in the fridge or for 3 hours at room temperature.

10. To serve, use the back of a spoon to schmear (see page 29) a quarter of the lemon mascarpone across the center of each of 4 plates. Place a Thai tea parfait in the center of each schmear. Sprinkle one-quarter of the Thai tea crunch over the center and down the sides of each parfait and top the crunch with tiny torn pieces of mint. Serve immediately.

lemon mascarpone

MAKES ABOUT 230 G (1 CUP)

Mascarpone cheese is a little fussy. It breaks really easily, so it is important here to make sure that both the lemon curd and the mascarpone are cold. Don't even think about overmixing this!

| ½ recipe | Lemon Curd (page 86) | |
| 50 g | mascarpone cheese | ¼ cup |

1. Put the lemon curd in the bowl of a stand mixer fitted with the paddle attachment and mix on medium-low speed to smooth it out a bit, about 30 seconds; scrape down the sides of the bowl with a spatula as necessary.

2. Add the mascarpone cheese and mix on low speed until just combined. You may need to mix the mascarpone in with a spatula at the very end to make sure it is evenly distributed without overmixing it. Use immediately, or store in an airtight container in the fridge for up to 1 week.

the ganache

Fall was approaching, and I wanted to put pumpkin on the menu in something other than a pie or ice cream, which are delicious but too easy. I wanted to do something new that would showcase pumpkin in a different light.

One afternoon at Milk Bar, I was flipping through one of the old notebooks I kept as a cook when I came upon a recipe for a sweet but savory squash filling we'd used, back when I worked for Alex Grunert at Bouley, to sandwich together macaroons. Bingo.

But how to make it my own, with a new texture and viscosity—something that was thick and voluptuous enough to stand alone on a plated dessert? I decided to start with the path of least resistance, a standard white chocolate ganache (melted white chocolate and butter blended with heavy cream). Then I added Libby's pumpkin puree, cinnamon, and some salt. It was *so* tasty, but I wanted it to have more texture, more body, and more pull, so I turned to my old friend, glucose.

Once the pumpkin ganache was a success, we ran with the technique and attempted a ganache with every root vegetable that could be roasted and pureed to mimic the consistency of pumpkin puree.

Because it's tough to market a squash cookie or a beet cake to the masses, who want cornflake-chocolate-chip-marshmallow cookies (and how can I blame them?), we love using this mother recipe to infuse splashes of seasonality in our kitchen, which is packed with cornflakes and mini chocolate chips year-round. The "ganache" gives us the opportunity to play with savory and sweet flavors deeper than just salt and sugar.

Though most of our ganaches are part of plated desserts for Ssäm Bar or Ko, there are plenty less fancy uses for any of these recipes. Pumpkin ganache is unbelievably tasty spread over the Oat Cookie (page 247), before it's turned into the crust for the crack pie, and served with Cereal Milk Ice Cream (page 38). It's also an amazing layer in the Carrot Layer Cake (page 117), replacing the graham frosting. (Or be a real hardbody, and make a carrot ganache using the mother recipe and layer it in the carrot cake in place of the graham frosting.)

Celery Root Ganache (page 209) and Tristar Strawberry Sorbet (page 216) make an amazing ice cream pie when layered into a Ritz Crunch crust (page 214). Or deconstruct the sorbet and celery root ganache dish and make it into a little dessert or snack, omitting the sorbet and lovage and using twice the amount of fresh berries; don't leave out the Ritz Crunch (page 53), though!

My go-to use for ganache—and my favorite way to make a pie look totally VIP—is to pipe ganache around the edges. My favorite, favorite, favorite pie that we make is the Blondie Pie (page 179), finished with pumpkin ganache. It makes a great fall/holiday dessert or gift. To get ganache on your pies, all you need is a pastry bag and some imagination. Star tip, regular tip—there's no limit to what you can do.

pumpkin ganache

MAKES ABOUT 340 G (1¼ CUPS)

This mother recipe is a breeze as long as you follow the steps and understand when ingredients are added and why. Melted together, the white chocolate and butter create a basic bond. The addition of glucose, needed for the texture it imparts, then breaks that bond. Cold heavy cream comes to the rescue, emulsifying the broken bond and forming a new, stronger bond. The pumpkin puree and seasonings are added last for flavor and additional body. Note that you *must* use a hand blender in this recipe, and for the other ganaches in this chapter.

150 g	white chocolate	5¼ ounces
25 g	butter	2 tablespoons
50 g	glucose	2 tablespoons
55 g	cold heavy cream	¼ cup
75 g	Libby's pumpkin puree	⅓ cup
4 g	kosher salt	1 teaspoon
1 g	ground cinnamon	½ teaspoon

In a pinch, substitute 18 g (1 tablespoon) corn syrup for the glucose.

1. Combine the white chocolate and butter in a microwave-safe dish and gently melt them in the microwave in 15-second bursts, stirring between blasts. The result should be barely warm to the touch and totally homogenous.

2. Transfer the chocolate mixture to a container that can accommodate an immersion blender—something tall and narrow, like a 1-quart plastic deli container. Warm the glucose in the microwave for 15 seconds, then immediately add to the chocolate mixture and buzz with the hand blender. After a minute, stream in the heavy cream, with the hand blender running—the mixture will come together into something silky, shiny, and smooth.

3. Blend in the pumpkin puree, salt, and cinnamon. Put the ganache in the fridge to firm up before using, at least 4 hours, or, ideally, overnight. Stored in an airtight container, pumpkin ganache will keep fresh in the fridge for 1 week. Serve cold.

celery root ganache

MAKES ABOUT 375 G (1½ CUPS)

Believe me, I had never even had celery root, let alone become infatuated with it, before we started experimenting with root vegetable ganaches. But, in case you haven't got the point by now, you can trust me on all sweet things that are delicious. I'm not trying to throw a nasty curve ball your way.

1 medium	celery root, peeled and cut into chunks	
10 g	grapeseed oil	1 tablespoon
1 g	kosher salt	¼ teaspoon
1 g	freshly ground black pepper	¼ teaspoon
	milk if needed	
150 g	white chocolate	5¼ ounces
40 g	butter	3 tablespoons
50 g	glucose	2 tablespoons
55 g	cold heavy cream	¼ cup
4 g	kosher salt	1 teaspoon

In a pinch, substitute 35 g (2 tablespoons) corn syrup for the glucose.

1. Heat the oven to 325°F.

2. Put the celery root chunks on a big sheet of aluminum foil. Add the oil, salt, and pepper and toss to coat the celery root. Fold up the foil to enclose the celery root, put the foil packet on a sheet pan for easy handling, and roast for 30 to 60 minutes. The celery root should be slightly caramelized and mushy-tender at that point; if not, give it additional 15-minute intervals in the oven.

3. Transfer the celery root to a blender and puree it. (If your blender is giving you trouble, add up to 2 tablespoons milk to help get it going.) Pass the puree through a fine-mesh strainer—it should have the texture of Libby's pumpkin puree (or baby food). Measure out 125 g (½ cup) celery root puree. Let cool.

4. Combine the white chocolate and butter in a microwave-safe dish and gently melt them in the microwave in 15-second bursts, stirring between blasts. The result should be barely warm to the touch and totally homogenous.

recipe continues

5. Transfer the chocolate mixture to a container that can accommodate an immersion blender—something tall and narrow, like a 1-quart plastic deli container. Warm the glucose in the microwave for 15 seconds, then immediately add to the chocolate mixture and buzz with the hand blender. After a minute, stream in the heavy cream, with the hand blender running—the mixture will come together into something silky, shiny, and smooth.

6. Blend in the celery root puree and salt; taste and add more salt if needed (due to the fresh, seasonal nature of celery root). Put the ganache in the fridge to firm up before using, at least 4 hours, or, ideally, overnight. Stored in an airtight container, it will keep in the fridge for 1 week. Serve cold.

beet-lime ganache

MAKES ABOUT 330 G (1½ CUPS)

This one is for the beet lovers out there. It's also for the not beet lovers out there. I am not a beet lover, but this ganache is delightful.

2	medium beets, peeled and cut into chunks (use gloves; see page 23)	
1	lime	
	milk if needed	
120 g	white chocolate	4¼ ounces
25 g	butter	2 tablespoons
100 g	glucose	¼ cup
55 g	cold heavy cream	¼ cup
3 g	kosher salt	¾ teaspoon

In a pinch, substitute 35 g (2 tablespoons) corn syrup for the glucose.

1. Heat the oven to 325°F.

2. Wrap the beet chunks up in a big sheet of aluminum foil and put on a sheet pan for easy handling. Roast for 1 to 2 hours, or until the beets are on the mushy side of tender; give them additional 30-minute intervals in the oven if they aren't.

3. Meanwhile, grate the zest from the lime; reserve. Squeeze 8 g (2 teaspoons) juice from the lime and reserve.

4. Transfer the beets to a blender and puree them. (If your blender is giving you trouble, add up to 1 tablespoon milk to help get it going.) Pass the puree through a fine-mesh strainer—it should have the texture of Libby's pumpkin puree (or baby food). Measure out 120 g (⅓ cup) beet puree. Let cool.

5. Combine the white chocolate and butter in a microwave-safe dish and gently melt them in the microwave in 15-second bursts, stirring between blasts. The result should be barely warm to the touch and totally homogenous.

6. Transfer the chocolate mixture to a container that can accommodate an immersion blender—something tall and narrow, like a 1-quart plastic deli container. Warm the glucose in the microwave for 15 seconds, then immediately add to the chocolate mixture and buzz with the hand blender. After a minute, stream in the heavy cream, with the hand blender running—the mixture will come together into something silky, shiny, and smooth.

7. Blend in the beet puree, lime zest, and salt. Put the ganache in the fridge for 30 minutes to firm up.

8. Use a spatula to fold the lime juice into the ganache (do not do this until the ganache is set, or you will break the ganache). Put the ganache back in the fridge for at least 3 hours, or, ideally, overnight. Stored in an airtight container, it will keep in the fridge for 1 week. Serve cold.

pear sorbet stilton, cornflake crunch, pumpkin ganache

SERVES 4

This is our take on a somewhat composed cheese dessert for Ssäm Bar.

½ recipe	Pumpkin Ganache (page 208)	
¼ recipe	Cornflake Crunch (page 51)	90 g (1 cup)
200 g	Stilton cheese, crumbled	7 ounces (1 cup)
1 recipe	Pear Sorbet (recipe follows)	

Schmear (see page 29) the ganache across 4 small dessert plates or up the sides of bowls. Create a small pile of the crunch just off the center of each dish. Top with the Stilton. Carefully perch generous scoops or quenelles (see page 28) of pear sorbet on top of the cheese. Serve at once.

pear sorbet

MAKES ABOUT 480 G (1 PINT)

1	gelatin sheet	
400 g	pear puree	2⅓ cups
50 g	glucose	2 tablespoons
30 g	elderflower cordial	1 tablespoon
0.5 g	kosher salt	⅛ teaspoon
0.5 g	citric acid (see page 16)	⅛ teaspoon

1. Bloom the gelatin (see page 29).

2. Warm a little bit of the pear puree and whisk in the gelatin to dissolve. Whisk in the remaining pear puree, the glucose, elderflower cordial, salt, and citric acid until everything is fully dissolved and incorporated.

3. Pour the mixture into your ice cream machine and freeze according to the manufacturer's instructions. The sorbet is best spun just before serving or using, but it will keep in an airtight container in the freezer for up to 2 weeks.

We use Poire William puree and elderflower cordial in this recipe; both are easily found at amazon.com.

With all things fresh and seasonal, it's always important to taste, taste, taste. Make the sorbet base to your liking with more glucose, salt, or citric acid (see page 26).

Powdered gelatin can be substituted for the sheet gelatin: use ½ teaspoon. In a pinch, substitute 18 g (1 tablespoon) corn syrup for the glucose.

tristar strawberry sorbet
macerated strawberries, lovage, ritz crunch, celery root ganache

SERVES 4

The tristar strawberry, pear sorbet, and goat froyo desserts are variations on a theme. Every pastry chef and department has a successful formula to piece flavors and textures together into desserts. This is ours: ganache + sorbet + textural element = plated dessert. These types of desserts highlight the way that Milk Bar components, which might seem kind of jokey (like Ritz crunch) or weird (like pumpkin ganache), can be brought together in unexpected ways as thoughtful, delicious, grown-up desserts.

The composition of these dishes can be looked at as guides for ways to put together fancy-looking plates at home. If you are baking out of this book a bunch—making liquid cheesecake or crunches or cakes and ending up with leftovers—you will see that plates like these are actually quite easy to assemble just from your scraps.

Think of these recipes as your Milk Bar final exam for all things sweet yet savory. Bonus points if you use chilled plates to serve the desserts.

Tristar strawberries are little gems from heaven. They are our favorite breed of strawberry, the hot commodity, if you will, for any pastry chef strolling through the Union Square farmers' market in search of seasonal revelation. Known for their unbelievably deep flavor and color, the tristars we hoard all summer long are from Rick Bishop at Mountain Sweet Berry Farm in Roscoe, New York.

1 recipe	Celery Root Ganache (page 209)
½ recipe	Ritz Crunch (page 53)
1 recipe	Macerated Strawberries with Lovage (recipe follows)
1 recipe	Tristar Strawberry Sorbet (recipe follows)

Schmear (see page 29) the ganache across 4 small dessert plates or up the sides of bowls. Scatter the crunch about the ganache. Arrange 8 to 10 strawberries around and on the schmear, leaving room in the middle for a generous scoop or quenelle (see page 28) of strawberry sorbet on each plate. Serve at once.

macerated strawberries with lovage

MAKES ABOUT 160 G (1½ CUPS)

Lovage looks like a young celery branch with leaves, and in fact tastes like a slightly spicy celery. Most farmers' markets have it in the spring and summer. Substitute a celery branch for the lovage stem in a pinch.

150 g	Tristar strawberries, hulled	1 pint
½ branch	lovage stem, chopped	
12 g	sugar	1 tablespoon
0.5 g	kosher salt	⅛ teaspoon
1 g	sherry vinegar	¼ teaspoon

Combine the strawberries, lovage, sugar, salt, and vinegar in a small bowl. Gently toss with a spoon until the strawberries are evenly coated. Cover and place in the fridge for at least 2 hours, or up to 2 days, before serving.

tristar strawberry sorbet

MAKES ABOUT 400 G (1 PINT)

Powdered gelatin can be substituted for the sheet gelatin: use ½ teaspoon. In a pinch, substitute 18 g (1 tablespoon) corn syrup for the glucose.

300 g	Tristar strawberries, hulled	2 pints
1	gelatin sheet	
50 g	glucose	2 tablespoons
25 g	sugar	2 tablespoons
0.5 g	kosher salt	⅛ teaspoon
0.5 g	citric acid (see page 16)	⅛ teaspoon

1. Puree the strawberries in a blender. Strain the puree through a fine-mesh sieve into a bowl to strain out the pips.

2. Bloom the gelatin (see page 29).

3. Warm a little bit of the strawberry puree and whisk in the gelatin to dissolve. Whisk in the remaining strawberry puree, the glucose, sugar, salt, and citric acid until everything is fully dissolved and incorporated.

4. Pour the mixture into your ice cream machine and freeze according to the manufacturer's instructions. The sorbet is best spun just before serving or using, but it will keep in an airtight container in the freezer for up to 2 weeks.

chèvre frozen yogurt
pistachio crunch, beet-lime ganache

SERVES 4

1 recipe	Beet-Lime Ganache (page 210)
½ recipe	Pistachio Crunch (page 186)
1 recipe	Chèvre Frozen Yogurt (recipe follows)

Schmear (see page 29) the ganache across 4 small dessert plates or up the sides of bowls. Scatter the crunch about the ganache. Scoop or quenelle (see page 28) the frozen yogurt and anchor it on the crunch. Serve at once.

chèvre frozen yogurt

MAKES ABOUT 400 G (1 PINT)

2	gelatin sheets	
55 g	milk	¼ cup
60 g	fresh chèvre	¼ cup
55 g	buttermilk	¼ cup
50 g	yogurt	2 tablespoons
100 g	glucose	¼ cup
50 g	sugar	¼ cup
2 g	kosher salt	½ teaspoon
0.5 g	citric acid (see page 16)	⅛ teaspoon

Powdered gelatin can be substituted for the sheet gelatin: use 1 teaspoon. In a pinch, substitute 35 g (2 tablespoons) corn syrup for the glucose.

1. Bloom the gelatin (see page 29).

2. Warm a little bit of the milk and whisk in the gelatin to dissolve. Transfer to a blender and add the remaining milk, the chèvre, buttermilk, yogurt, glucose, sugar, salt, and citric acid. Puree until smooth.

3. Pour the base through a fine-mesh strainer into your ice cream machine and freeze according to the manufacturer's instructions. The frozen yogurt is best spun just before serving or using, but it will keep in an airtight container in the freezer for up to 2 weeks.

mother

dough

When we first opened Milk Bar, we were more than just Milk Bar: we called ourselves Momofuku Milk Bar & Bakery. We wanted to be both an early morning stop for fresh, crunchy, artisan bread made right and the modern-day Milk Bar with a point of view on sweets. With James Mark, an aspiring master bread baker, at the helm, we made the executive decision that what we really needed to do was to fill our tiny space with huge deck ovens, the kind pro bread bakers use.

Those deck ovens took up all of our precious real estate. We had to wiggle by each other. And they were only ever on and in use for an hour or two a day. We probably made $100 a day off the breads that came out of them, while the little countertop-fridge-turned-pork-bun-station next to it, which took up one-tenth of the space, churned and burned like a true moneymaker all day and all night.

We needed to make a change, both to our space and to our loosely based ideas on what we wanted to be and the food we wanted to serve.

Every busy night, we had blue cheese polenta bread loaves left over, but we stayed late making the steamed bun dough for pork buns. We had to start thinking about our bread program in the same way we thought about our sweet baked goods.

How far could we take that steamed dough recipe? From a classic approach to bread baking, a basic dough can be shaped, proofed, and baked in a number of different ways. In a French kitchen, a baguette and a *pain d'épi* both come from the same rustic dough. So, why not a steamed bun, a loaf of brioche, and a croissant made from the same dough in the kitchen at Milk Bar?

So we began experimenting. The bun dough was wet but firm, easy to mix and shape—in a word, reliable. We brainstormed our family favorite breads: focaccia, bagels, croissants, cinnamon buns. Then we made them with the steamed bun dough as the starting point. Some of the recipes converged with classic Momofuku flavors, like miso, pork, or kimchi. Others we stuffed with our favorite cream cheese spread or deli meats.

Our bread program finally took off. The deck ovens, however, are long gone. We used the space for more refrigeration for those damn cookies and an additional area to roll out bread or assemble cakes or layer cinnamon bun pies, depending on our production needs at any given time of day. Now that we've moved to our Brooklyn kingdom, that old space houses extra soft-serve base and a larger pork-bun-and-pickle station for Ssäm Bar. One day, those few square feet may even turn into a plain old hard bar. But for us, those few square feet of real estate will always be the homeland of the mother dough.

mother dough

MAKES ABOUT 850 G (2 POUNDS)

The cakes, cookies, or pies may have lured you into this book, but you are about to meet your favorite recipe. This bread dough is always tasty, *very* forgiving, and can be fashioned into nearly any style or variety of bready item. It takes a very "don't take yourself so seriously!" approach to bread baking and is the easiest, most versatile recipe in the book—your resulting bagel bombs, volcanoes, brioche, focaccia, and croissants will be proof of that.

Make this dough one day, refrigerate it, and use it the second, third, or fourth day, if need be. Or freeze it for up to 1 week; just make sure to let it come to room temperature before using.

Elsewhere in this book: Mother dough is used in Cinnamon Bun Pie (page 152).

550 g	flour	3½ cups
12 g	kosher salt	1 tablespoon
3.5 g	active dry yeast	½ packet or 1⅛ teaspoons
370 g	water, at room temperature	1¾ cups

grapeseed oil

1. Stir together the flour, salt, and yeast in the bowl of your stand mixer—do it by hand, using the dough hook like a spoon. Continue stirring by hand as you add the water, mixing for 1 minute, until the mixture has come together into a shaggy mass.

2. Engage the bowl and hook and have the machine mix the dough on the lowest speed for 3 minutes, or until the ball of dough is smoother and more cohesive. Then knead for 4 more minutes on the lowest speed. The dough should look like a wet ball and should bounce back softly when prodded.

3. Brush a large bowl with oil and dump the dough into it. Cover with plastic wrap and let the dough proof at room temperature for 45 minutes.

4. The dough is ready to be used as directed in the following recipes. If you do not plan to use your mother dough the day you make it, you can store it in an airtight container at least twice its size in the fridge for up to 3 days. Take it out of the fridge and let it come to room temperature 30 to 45 minutes before using.

bagel bombs

½ recipe	Mother Dough (opposite), proofed	
1 recipe	Bacon, Scallion, Cream Cheese Plugs (recipe follows), frozen	
1	egg	
4 g	water	½ teaspoon
1 recipe	Everything Bagel Mix (recipe follows)	

1. Heat the oven to 325°F.

2. Punch down and flatten the dough on a smooth, dry countertop. Use a dough cutter to divide the dough into 8 equal pieces. Use your fingers to gently stretch each piece of dough out into a mini pizza between 2 and 3 inches wide.

3. Put a cream cheese plug in the center of each dough circle. Bring up the edges of each round and pinch to seal so that the cream cheese plug is completely contained, then gently roll the ball between the palms of your hands to ensure the bomb has a nice, round, dinner roll–y shape. Arrange the bombs 4 inches apart on a parchment- or Silpat-lined baking sheet.

4. Whisk the egg and water together and brush a generous coat of egg wash on the buns. Sprinkle a heavy even coating of the bagel mix all over the bagel bombs—every possible inch, except for the bottoms, should be coated.

5. Bake the bagel bombs for 20 to 30 minutes. While in the oven, the bombs will become a deep golden brown and a few may have cream cheese explosions. Continue baking until you see this happen! Not to worry—serve them as is or use your fingers to tuck the cream cheese back inside the bagel bomb. Bagel bombs are best served warm out of the oven—or flashed in the oven later to warm and serve. If you can't finish them all right away, once they are cool, wrap them well in plastic and store them in the fridge for up to 3 days.

bacon, scallion, cream cheese plugs

MAKES ENOUGH FOR 1 RECIPE BAGEL BOMBS

We use Benton's bacon, the meatiest, smokiest bacon around, in our plugs. If you have the Momofuku cookbook, you know the wonders and glories of Allan Benton, the man behind the smoky cured pork down in Madisonville, Tennessee. His product reigns supreme in punch-you-in-the-face bacon flavor. When he answers the phone himself to take your order, you know you are getting a handmade, superior product from a man who loves his art and keeps it simple—even though he has orders from all over the country to fill that day, many from big-name chefs and restaurants in NYC and beyond. I have been known to swap cookies for moonshine with this adorable man—both of us feeling like we've made out like bandits.

Make a meat-free cream cheese plug with your favorite bagal fixin's. We make a veggie plug with dill and cucumber, too!

50 g	bacon, the smokier the better	1¾ ounces
200 g	cream cheese	7 ounces
2 g	scallion greens, thinly sliced	
5 g	sugar	1 teaspoon
2 g	kosher salt	½ teaspoon

1. Cook the bacon in a skillet over medium heat until it's auburn brown and crunchy. Remove it from the pan and chop it into small pieces; reserve it and, separately, the bacon fat in the pan.

2. Put the cream cheese in the bowl of a stand mixer fitted with the paddle attachment and cream it on medium speed. Pour in the reserved bacon fat and paddle to combine. Scrape down the sides of the bowl. Add the chopped bacon, scallions, sugar, and salt and paddle briefly to incorporate.

3. Scoop the cream cheese mixture onto a quarter sheet pan in 8 even lumps. Freeze until rock hard, 1 to 3 hours.

4. Once the plugs are frozen solid, they are ready to be used, or they can be stored in an airtight container in the freezer for up to 1 month.

everything bagel mix

MAKES ENOUGH FOR 1 RECIPE BAGEL BOMBS

3 g	kosher salt	¾ teaspoon
6 g	white sesame seeds	1 tablespoon
4 g	black sesame seeds	2 teaspoons
4 g	poppy seeds	2 teaspoons
4 g	dried onions	1 tablespoon
2 g	onion powder	½ teaspoon
1 g	garlic powder	¼ teaspoon

Mix together the salt, sesame seeds, poppy seeds, dried onions, onion powder, and garlic powder in an airtight container. The mix keeps forever in the pantry, but it is best used within 6 months.

volcanoes

MAKES 4 VOLCANOES

In February 2008, I traveled with Dave to Deauville, France, for the third annual Omnivore Food Festival. The two of us were like fish out of water in this off-season beach town. Straight off the plane from New York and jet-lagged, we were left to our own devices in the tiny, remote town to gather Asian ingredients for a kimchi demo.

We agreed to wake up at 6 a.m. the next day to get breakfast and get going. We met drowsy and confused in the empty hotel lobby and proceeded to sleepwalk through the ghost town until we could smell fresh-baked bread and saw a light on in the only bakery in town. Dave took charge and pointed at nearly everything in the joint, as that's how we eat when we're abroad. "I'm full" is not a phrase you're allowed to use—such is the price of traveling with chef Dave Chang.

We found a bench outside and unwrapped this mound of bread that looked like it had some sort of creamy gravy inside. Still half-asleep, we wrestled the filled bread ball out of the bag and bit in. When you are having a food moment, it's like tasting food for the first time. Your eyes open wide and then close, as if in slow motion. You chew as if no food with flavor has ever touched your tongue before and what you are eating at that very moment is what will shape all future food opinions you will ever have. That was our 6:05 a.m. February morning in Deauville. Neither of us speaks French, so we decided to call it what it was, a volcano—an explosion of potato, lardons, and cheese like no other. We raced each other to the bakery every subsequent morning that week. And on the plane ride home, we agreed that if and when we opened a bakery, it *must* serve our very own volcano.

½ recipe	Mother Dough (page 222), proofed	
1 recipe	Caramelized Onions (recipe follows)	
1 recipe	Scalloped Potatoes (recipe follows)	
1	egg	
4 g	water	½ teaspoon
100 g	shredded Gruyère cheese	3.5 ounces (1 cup)

1. Heat the oven to 375°F.

2. Punch down and flatten the dough on a smooth, dry countertop. Use a dough cutter to divide the dough into 4 equal pieces. Use your fingers to gently stretch each piece of dough out into a mini pizza about 6 inches wide.

3. Divide the onions equally among the rounds, plopping them in the center. Grab the scalloped potatoes from the fridge and cut into four 3-inch squares. Use an offset spatula to wrestle each square of potato gratin out of the baking pan and onto a dough round, directly on top of the onions.

4. Take the edges of each dough round and pinch together to seal so that there is no speck of onion or potato in sight, then gently roll the ball between the palms of your hands to ensure the volcano has a nice, round, dinner roll–y shape. Arrange the volcanoes, seam side down, 5 inches apart on a parchment- or Silpat-lined baking sheet.

5. Whisk the egg and water together and brush a generous coat of egg wash on the buns. Use a paring knife to cut a 1-inch-long X in the top of each volcano. Divide the Gruyère evenly among the volcanoes, stuffing it into the X in each one.

6. Bake the volcanoes for 25 minutes, or until the dough is a deep, golden brown and the Gruyère cheese on top is caramelized. They are best served warm; allow them to cool for at least 10 minutes before digging in. If you're saving a couple of volcanoes for later, let them cool, wrap them well in plastic, and store them in the fridge for up to 3 days; warm them in the oven before eating.

caramelized onions

MAKES ENOUGH FOR 1 RECIPE VOLCANOES

I love caramelized onions. I make them constantly at home and put them in everything from sandwiches to nachos piled high to scrambled eggs. They add a roasted depth of flavor and an unbelievable sweetness.

20 g	grapeseed oil	2 tablespoons
2	medium Spanish onions, halved and thinly sliced	
6 g	kosher salt	1½ teaspoons

1. Heat the oil in a large heavy-bottomed pan or skillet over medium-high heat for 1 minute, or until it's very hot but not smoking. Add the onions and let them cook for 2 to 3 minutes without stirring.

2. Toss the onions with a large spoon or spatula while seasoning them with the salt. Lower the heat to medium-low. The rest of the caramelization process happens slowly over medium-low heat for 20 minutes. Work on another subrecipe, pay some bills, kill some time productively—but don't go too far from the onions. Toss the onions over on themselves every 3 to 4 minutes so they all get their time on the bottom of the pan. The onions will weep and then slowly take on color as they release their liquid. When your onions are the color of a brown paper bag, they are done. Cool completely before using in the volcanoes, or store in an airtight container in the fridge for up to 1 week.

scalloped potatoes

MAKES ENOUGH FOR 1 RECIPE VOLCANOES

1	garlic clove		
105 g	heavy cream	½ cup	
85 g	milk	⅓ cup	
½	bay leaf		
¼	rosemary sprig		
2 g	kosher salt	½ teaspoon	
0.5 g	freshly ground black pepper	pinch	
80 g	pancetta	3 ounces	
2	russet (baking) potatoes		

1. Smash the garlic clove with the palm of your hand and remove the skin. Put the garlic in a small saucepan with the cream, milk, bay leaf, rosemary, salt, and pepper and bring to a simmer over low heat, then take the saucepan off the heat, cover, and let steep for 30 minutes. The cream mixture will seem strong and overseasoned, but it will eventually season all of the scalloped potatoes, so don't freak out.

2. Meanwhile, cut the pancetta into ½-inch cubes. Brown it in a small saucepan over medium heat. You want to caramelize and cook the pancetta slightly, to increase its presence later in the scalloped potatoes. Set aside.

3. Peel the potatoes and slice just thicker than paper-thin slices, about ⅛ inch thick. Submerge them in a bowl of cold water.

4. Heat the oven to 350°F. Pull out a 6-inch square baking pan (if you don't have one, you can buy a disposable one at the grocery).

5. Layer the potatoes in the pan like shingles, putting bits of browned pancetta between each layer of potato shingles, until you are out of both potatoes and pancetta. Fish out the herbs and garlic clove from the steeped cream mixture with a slotted or regular spoon, and pour it over the potatoes.

6. Bake for 45 minutes, or until the potatoes on top are golden brown and have a milky translucence but have not burned or turned into potato chips.

7. Cool and chill the scalloped potatoes in the fridge for 2 to 3 hours, covered with plastic and with a bowl of leftovers weighting them down and keeping every shingle tight and condensed in the pan.

8. Use in the volcano once cool. To store for later use, take the weights off, wrap the scalloped potatoes especially well in plastic, and return to the fridge for up to 5 days.

kimchi & blue cheese croissants

MAKES 5 CROISSANTS

This is the first croissant we ever made and sold at Milk Bar. Deeply stinky and pungent in all the right ways, it is not for the faint of heart. It is a true marriage of funky, barnyardy, stringent kimchi and blue cheese, of our Korean roots to our Italian ones. It is for our soul sisters and brothers.

Making croissants is one of the coolest bread techniques around. You spend time making many layers of bread dough and butter, folding and turning the dough all along. When baked, the croissants get their flakiness and volume from the steam that the layers of butter give off as the dough heats. The steam separates each dough layer ever so slightly, resulting in this massively puffy, impossibly flaky creation. And when you make them with a flavored butter, they're even cooler!

Though we have simplified the technique somewhat at Milk Bar, in terms of speed and precision, this recipe is still not for softbodies. It takes more time with the dough, more flour, more time with the rolling pin. But it will make you feel like a true pro when the oven timer goes off and you pull these bad boys out.

½ recipe	Mother Dough (page 222), proofed	
105 g	flour, for dusting	⅔ cup
1 recipe	Kimchi Butter (recipe follows)	
200 g	blue cheese, crumbled	7 ounces (1 cup)
1	egg	
4 g	water	½ teaspoon

1. Punch down and flatten the dough on a smooth, dry countertop. Dust the counter, the dough, and a rolling pin with flour, and roll out the dough to a rectangle about 8 × 12 inches and even in thickness. Grab the butter pad from the fridge and place it on one half of the dough rectangle. Fold the other half of the dough rectangle over the butter pad and pinch the edges shut around it. Drape with plastic wrap and let rest for 10 minutes at room temperature.

2. To make the croissants, you will need to put 3 "double book" turns into the dough to create enough alternating layers of flour and butter to make the

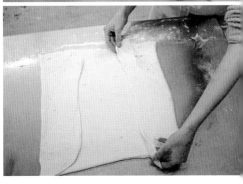

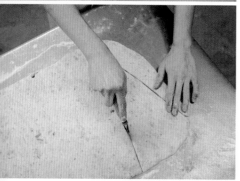

croissants rise and puff in the oven. To make your first double book turn, dust your counter surface, your rolling pin, and the dough with flour, remembering to dust under the dough as well. Roll the dough out again to a rectangle 8 × 12 inches and even in thickness. Be gentle with the rolling pin, making sure not to break into any part of the butter bundle or roll so hard that the butter rolls right out of the dough. (If this happens, push it back in and pull a little dough over the escape hole to patch it up.) Make sure there is not an excessive amount of flour left on or underneath your dough—dust off any excess with your hands.

3. Visually divide your dough lengthwise into quarters. Fold the two outer quarters over to the center axis, or spine, of the rectangle of dough, so they meet in the center. Then close the book, bringing one edge to meet the other with the spine now to one side. (When I'm showing someone how to make a double book turn, I stretch my monkey arms out wide like I'm going in for a big hug, then I fold my arms at the elbow, so my fingers are touching my armpits, and fold my elbows in to touch one another. That is what your dough should look like. Book turn complete.) Wrap it loosely in plastic and transfer it to the fridge for 30 minutes.

4. Repeat steps 2 and 3 twice more to make a total of 3 turns,. Each time you start a turn, make sure to have the open edges, or seam, of your dough facing away from you. Sometimes we write 1, 2, or 3 on the plastic we use to wrap the dough as we are putting the turns into it so we don't lose count. If you put in one too many turns, it will not hurt your dough; if you skip one, you will end up very disappointed in your softbody croissants.

5. For your last and final roll-out, dust your counter surface, your rolling pin, and your dough with flour, remembering to dust under the dough as well. Roll the dough out to a rectangle that's 8 × 12 inches and even in thickness.

6. With a paring knife or a pizza cutter, cut the dough into 5 triangles, each 8 inches long from the pointiest tip to the center of the side across it and 4 inches wide at the bottom. You should have 5 triangles (2 upside down and 3 right side up) plus some scrap on the right and left. Divide the blue cheese among the croissants, putting it into the center of the wide bottom end of each triangle. Starting at the blue cheese end, use one hand to begin rolling the dough toward the tip of the triangle while your other hand holds the tip and gently stretches it away. Continue until the triangle is completely rolled up into a crescent shape. Make sure the tip of the triangle is tucked underneath the body of the crescent, or it will unravel in the oven. Roll the scraps up into kimchi croissant knots or make baby pigs in blankets!

7. Transfer the croissants to a parchment-lined sheet pan, arranging them 6 inches apart. Cover lightly with plastic and leave at room temperature to double in size, about 45 minutes.

8. Heat the oven to 375°F.

9. Whisk the egg and water together in a small bowl. Generously coat the top of your croissants with the egg wash, using a brush.

10. Bake the croissants for 20 to 25 minutes, or until they double in size, caramelize on the edges, and have a crusty outer layer that sounds hollow when you tap them. They're killer out of the oven and delicious at room temperature. If for some strange reason they don't get eaten immediately, wrap them individually in plastic and keep them refrigerated for up to 3 days. We like to toast our croissants before eating on the second and third days.

kimchi butter

MAKES ABOUT 205 G (1 CUP), OR ENOUGH FOR 1 BATCH KIMCHI & BLUE CHEESE CROISSANTS

Growing up, I hated this Korean fermented delicacy. My father would drag me miles away to the Korean supermarket down an alley to buy this stuff. He would bring it home and literally evacuate the house when he broke the seal on the jar. It wasn't until I started working at Momofuku that I learned that I really love kimchi, and that there are many, many levels of potency throughout the kimchi-producing kitchens in this country. The Momofuku cookbook has a ridiculously tasty kimchi recipe (among others). Or use your favorite brand of cabbage-based kimchi in this recipe.

90 g	kimchi	½ cup
115 g	butter, at room temperature	8 tablespoons (1 stick)
2 g	kosher salt	½ teaspoon
1 g	freshly ground black pepper	¼ teaspoon

1. Put the kimchi in a hand blender–friendly container and puree it.

2. Put the butter in the bowl of a stand mixer fitted with the paddle attachment and paddle on medium speed for 2 to 3 minutes, until light and fluffy. Scrape down the sides of the bowl. Add the pureed kimchi, salt, and pepper and paddle for another 2 minutes; the liquid from the kimchi will try and separate the butter during this time, but the paddling will keep it in line. When the mixture is light, fluffy, and red, stop and scrape down the sides of the bowl.

3. Turn the butter out onto a piece of parchment. Lay a second piece of parchment on top of it and press down on the butter with your hands to flatten it into a 4 × 6-inch rectangle. Transfer the butter-filled parchment to the fridge to firm up. Wrapped in plastic, the kimchi butter pad will keep fresh in the fridge for up to 1 month.

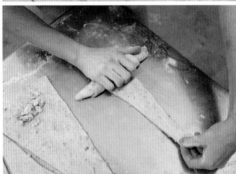

turkey, swiss & mustard croissants

MAKES 5 CROISSANTS

Have you ever had a turkey croissandwich on an airplane, or in a country club, or at a catered corporate event? The ones made with mass-produced croissants and stuffed with turkey cut in half? We always want to like them, but they're always so disappointing. So we came up with one we love.

The mustard croissant is very similar to the kimchi croissant in technique, but it is stuffed with meat, cheese, and condiments instead of blue cheese. You can substitute your favorite meat-and-cheese sandwich combo, if you prefer, for the turkey and Swiss.

½ recipe	Mother Dough (page 222), proofed	
105 g	flour, for dusting	⅔ cup
1 recipe	Mustard Butter (recipe follows)	
130 g	sliced turkey	5 ounces
70 g	shredded Swiss cheese	2½ ounces (¾ cup)
20 g	mayonnaise	2 tablespoons
1	egg	
4 g	water	½ teaspoon

1. Follow the recipe for the Kimchi Croissants (page 231) through step 5, substituting the mustard butter for the kimchi butter.

2. With a paring knife or a pizza cutter, cut the dough into 5 triangles, each 8 inches long from the pointiest tip to the center of the side across it and 4 inches wide at the bottom. Divide the sliced turkey among the 5 croissants, stacking the slices onto the center of the wide bottom end of the triangle. Arrange the Swiss cheese on top of the turkey, using your fingers to form it into nests. Dollop the mayonnaise into the Swiss cheese nests.

3. Starting at the wide bottom end, use one hand to begin rolling the dough toward the tip of the triangle while your other hand holds the tip and gently stretches it away. Continue until the triangle is completely rolled up into a crescent shape. Make sure the tip of the triangle is tucked underneath the body of the crescent, or it will unravel in the oven. Roll the scraps into mustard knots or make baby pigs in blankets!

4. Transfer the croissants to a parchment-lined sheet pan, arranging them 6 inches apart. Cover lightly with plastic and leave at room temperature to double in size, about 45 minutes.

5. Heat the oven to 375°F.

6. Whisk the egg and water together in a small bowl. Generously coat the top of your croissants with the egg wash, using a brush.

7. Bake the croissants for 20 to 25 minutes, or until they double in size, caramelize on the edges, and have a crusty outer layer that sounds hollow when you tap them. They're killer out of the oven and delicious at room temperature. If for some strange reason they don't get eaten immediately, wrap them individually in plastic and keep them refrigerated for up to 3 days. We like to toast our croissants before eating on the second and third days.

mustard butter

MAKES 180 G (¾ CUP), OR ENOUGH FOR 1 BATCH OF TURKEY, SWISS & MUSTARD CROISSANTS

This butter is great on a soft pretzel, a warm sandwich, or a hot dog bun!

115 g	butter, at room temperature	8 tablespoons (1 stick)
25 g	yellow mustard, such as French's	1 teaspoon
8 g	sherry vinegar	2 teaspoons
2 g	Worcestershire sauce	½ teaspoon
25 g	sugar	2 tablespoons
8 g	kosher salt	2 teaspoons

1. Put the butter in the bowl of a stand mixer fitted with the paddle attachment and paddle, on medium speed for 2 to 3 minutes, until fluffy and light yellow. Add the mustard, vinegar, Worcestershire, sugar, and salt and mix for another 2 to 3 minutes. Scrape down the sides of the bowl and mix for an additional minute. Make the butter pad as described below for the croissants, or store the butter in an airtight container in the fridge for up to 1 month.

2. To make the butter pad, turn the butter out onto a piece of parchment. Lay a second piece of parchment on top of it and press down on the butter with your hands to flatten it into a 4 × 6-inch rectangle. Transfer the butter-filled parchment to the fridge to firm up. Wrapped in plastic, the mustard butter pad will keep fresh in the fridge for up to 1 month.

black pepper brioche

MAKES 1 (8 × 4-INCH) LOAF

Black pepper brioche makes killer club sandwich bread or savory bread pudding. It also makes a mean sandwich with Thanksgiving or Christmas leftovers.

There are plenty of elaborate ways to form a loaf of bread, and even more intricate ways to form a loaf of brioche, but it all tastes the same, and you've already cheated death by using the mother dough, so we're going to take it easy on the loaf-forming lecture. Take the ice cream scoop you use for cookies and use it to scoop rounds of the dough into a loaf pan.

This is probably the most sacrilegious "brioche" recipe you will ever find. But stop taking yourself so seriously. Paddle the butter into the dough and bake the damn thing and enjoy.

If you're not a black pepper fan, shame on you. Replace the black pepper butter with any other butter you love. Use caraway seeds in place of black pepper. Or ground cinnamon, etc. Or use the Kimchi Butter (page 233) or Mustard Butter (page 235).

1 recipe	Mother Dough (page 222), proofed	
1 recipe	Black Pepper Butter (recipe follows), at room temperature	
1	egg	
4 g	water	½ teaspoon

1. Punch down and flatten the dough on a smooth, dry countertop. Put the dough and butter in the bowl of a stand mixer fitted with the paddle attachment and knead on low speed for 2 to 3 minutes, or until the butter has been incorporated into the dough.

2. Using a 2¾-ounce cookie scoop, scoop the dough into a greased 8 × 4-inch loaf pan, 2 rounds wide and 3 rounds long, with 2 extra rounds centered on top. Cover with a piece of plastic and allow the dough to rise until doubled in size, about 1½ hours.

3. Heat the oven to 350°F.

4. Whisk the egg and water together in a small bowl. Using a brush, generously coat the top of your brioche with the egg wash.

5. Bake the bread for 35 to 45 minutes. Choose an inconspicuous angle to insert your instant-read thermometer into the center of the loaf—you don't want to leave a hole in the top of the loaf. The brioche is baked when it reaches 220°F. If you do not have a thermometer, use a skewer—if it comes out clean, with no signs or spots of doughiness, the brioche is done.

6. Cool the brioche loaf completely in the pan before eating it. (It will finish baking as it cools.) If you can't eat it all in one sitting, it will keep fresh, wrapped well in plastic, for up to 3 days at room temperature.

black pepper butter

MAKES ABOUT 275 G (1½ CUPS)

225 g	butter, at room temperature	16 tablespoons (2 sticks)
25 g	sugar	2 tablespoons
12 g	kosher salt	1 tablespoon
8 g	finely ground black pepper	2 teaspoons

Combine the butter, sugar, salt, and pepper in the bowl of a stand mixer fitted with the paddle attachment and mix on medium speed for 2 minutes, or until the butter is fluffy, the sugar is dissolved, and the mixture is homogenous. Scrape down the sides of the bowl and mix for an additional minute. Use immediately, or store in an airtight container in the fridge for up to 1 month.

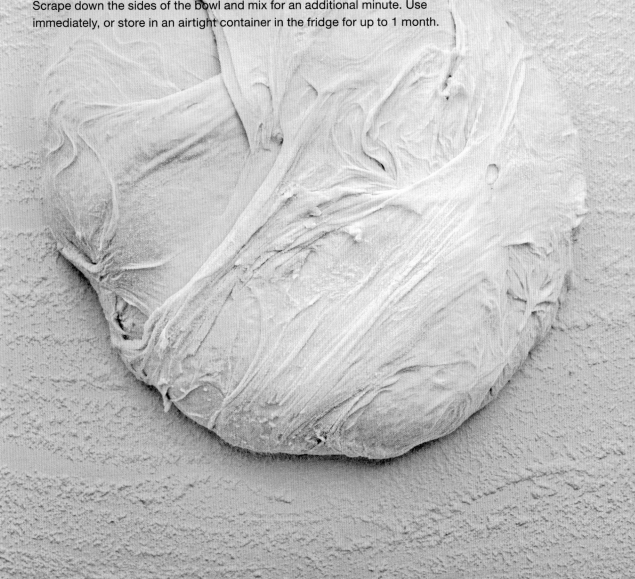

chinese sausage focaccia

MAKES 1 QUARTER SHEET PAN; SERVES 6

This focaccia is a favorite of many early Milk Bar regulars. It is the brainchild of our beloved James Mark and will go down in our history as the most delicious focaccia man has ever made.

340 g	Chinese sausages	12 ounces
8	garlic cloves	
150 g	grapeseed oil	1 cup
90 g	toban djan	⅓ cup
1 recipe	Mother Dough (page 222), proofed	

Feel free to substitute a mixture of shiro miso and a squirt or two of your favorite hot sauce for the toban djan (a Sichuan chile bean sauce). If both Chinese sausage *and* toban djan freak you out, you can substitute your favorite pepperoni and fresh or dried Italian seasonings in their place.

1. With a sharp knife, cut each Chinese sausage link lengthwise in half. Then slice each half into 12 half-moons. Cut the garlic cloves into thin slices on a bias—the thinner you can get them, the better.

2. Combine the oil, toban djan, sausage, and garlic in a saucepan and cook over medium-low heat for 15 minutes; the oil will turn a deep red color, the Chinese sausage will darken, and the garlic will become translucent. Strain the oil through a fine-mesh sieve into a bowl, saving it for later. Set the sausage aside.

3. Punch down and flatten the dough on a smooth, dry countertop. Stretch the dough out gently by hand until it is slightly longer and wider than a quarter sheet pan.

4. Visualize dividing your dough lengthwise in thirds. Spread half of the sausage and garlic down the center third of the dough. Fold the right third of dough over it. Cover that layer with the remaining sausage-garlic filling, then fold the left third of dough over.

5. Gently lift the dough at both ends and transfer to the baking pan. Cover loosely with plastic and allow it to rise at room temperature until doubled in size, about 45 minutes.

6. Heat the oven to 375°F.

7. Once the dough has doubled in size and has filled every bit of the baking pan, use your fingers to gently dimple the top of the dough to make small indentations. Pour the spicy garlic oil around, not on top of, the dough.

8. Bake for 15 minutes, or until the focaccia is golden brown.

9. Let the focaccia cool to room temperature in the pan before serving. If you attempt to cut into it while it is still hot or warm, it will seem gummy and underbaked.

10. Slice the focaccia into 6 pieces and serve at room temperature, or toast by flashing in a warm oven. The focaccia will remain delicious, wrapped well in plastic, for up to 3 days.

bonus track:

crack pie™

I love the *Joy of Cooking.* I've probably read it a million times, and I go back to it every time I'm searching for inspiration or a great story on how different food classics came to be. I'm the kind of person who will sit and listen to my grandma tell stories anytime, especially when they revolve around kitchen creations and kitchen disasters—which is probably the reason I became obsessed with the history of chess pie.

I've told this silly story so many times I feel like a broken record, describing something that really wasn't supposed to be the phenomenon that it became.

While working at wd~50, I decided to make it my goal to prepare family meal dessert once or more every day. Savory cooks have to do it daily, so why not pastry cooks too? It became a great exercise in making something out of nothing, or whatever mise-en-place was left over from the previous night's service. Everything at wd~50 was so precise, I used the twenty minutes at the beginning of my day to bake the way I baked at home—with reckless abandon, no measuring. It was my "me time." I took advantage of Wylie's wealth of cookbooks and taught myself to make classic baked goods that I'd never learned at home or in school. I eyeballed the ingredients and tasted and touched them raw and finished to better understand and practice the hows and whys of what too much flour, too little water, too many eggs, or too little baking soda tasted like and did to my latest family meal offering.

One Sunday morning as I was tying on my apron, I grabbed the *Joy of Cooking* and flipped through the pies to find something to base family meal dessert on. Thing is, it was a Sunday, and as I rifled through the fridge and the pages of the cookbook, I realized I didn't have much to work with. I actually had nothing interesting at all. That's when I came across the recipe for chess pie. Chess pie is the pie the old gals of yesteryear made when there was nothing to really make pie out of. When nothing was in season, the pantry void of all jars and cans from the harvest season before. Many down South called it "just pie," as opposed to cherry pie or apple pie, and down South the drawl is so severe, it was heard as "jesssss [silent t] pie," or "chess pie," or so the story goes. . . . How perfect, I thought.

I grabbed what I thought my chess pie ingredients should be. Since I loved gooey butter cake *so* much, that meant sugar, brown sugar (one of my favorite flavors), salt, butter, vanilla, egg yolks, and cream. The chess pie recipe in *Joy of Cooking* seemed to have some acidity by way of the buttermilk it called for, but I knew I wanted my pie to be rich and gooey, so I used heavy cream instead. The recipe also called for a little flour as a binder, but I wanted my pie to be a bit more interesting than that, so I used corn powder and milk powder, in the hopes they'd have the same setting effect on the body of the filling.

The pie went in the oven. I'd approached it like a baked custard, knowing that I didn't want the eggs to bake my pie into a firmer sweet quiche. But the pie's top colored quickly, and I was in a hurry that day to do my real job as a pastry cook, preparing for dinner service, so I pulled the pie a little earlier than I should have. The center was still plenty jiggly. I threw the warm pie in the fridge and starting banging out my prep list for the day.

When family meal came, I tucked my failed creation at the end of the smorgasbord, apologizing for what it was or was not. I had pretty much written off the underbaked pie until someone cut into it, took a bite, and started freaking out. Before I knew it, we were all huddled around it, taking bites and making noises. We instantly realized we needed to get that pie out of sight and out of mind, or we would eat the whole thing and that wouldn't bode well for the grueling seven-hour dinner service ahead.

I wrapped the gooey pie up, stuffed it in a lowboy, and jittered away. Minutes later, a cook, equally jittery, came up to me, looking for more pie. I gave it to him. Then another cook brought the pie back to me, begging me to take it away from him. Then another came for just one more bite. We shamelessly fought over the last bites of the pie. We soared high on sugar that evening. And then we crashed. It was awful. But that's the story of how crack pie got its name.

When it came time to make an opening menu for the bakery we'd call Milk Bar, it was clear that it would have to be a hodgepodge of baked goods that had followed me through life and that this was one of the musts. I made a salty, hearty oat crust to hold the buttery goodness just right. Crack pie quickly became a staple of our storefront. There's safety and camaraderie in numbers. My greatest feat was finding out I'm not the only one who can crush a whole crack pie—there's a city out there full of sweet-toothed soulmates.

crack pie™

This recipe makes two pies (two pies are always better than one), but you can always keep the second pie frozen if need be!

1 recipe	Oat Cookie (recipe follows)	
15 g	light brown sugar	1 tablespoon tightly packed
1 g	salt	¼ teaspoon
55 g	butter, melted, or as needed	4 tablespoons (½ stick)
1 recipe	Crack Pie Filling (recipe follows)	
	confectioners' sugar, for dusting	

1. Heat the oven to 350°F.

2. Put the oat cookie, brown sugar, and salt in a food processor and pulse it on and off until the cookie is broken down into a wet sand. (If you don't have a food processor, you can fake it till you make it and crumble the oat cookie diligently with your hands.)

3. Transfer the crumbs to a bowl, add the butter, and knead the butter and ground cookie mixture until moist enough to form into a ball. If it is not moist enough to do so, melt an additional 14 to 25 g (1 to 1½ tablespoons) butter and knead it in.

4. Divide the oat crust evenly between 2 (10-inch) pie tins. Using your fingers and the palms of your hands, press the oat cookie crust firmly into each pie tin, making sure the bottom and sides of the tin are evenly covered. Use the pie shells immediately, or wrap well in plastic and store at room temperature for up to 5 days or in the fridge for up to 2 weeks.

5. Put both pie shells on a sheet pan. Divide the crack pie filling evenly between the crusts; the filling should fill them three-quarters of the way full. Bake for 15 minutes only. The pies should be golden brown on top but will still be very jiggly.

6. Open the oven door and reduce the oven temperature to 325°F. Depending on your oven, it may take 5 minutes or longer for the oven to cool to the new temperature. Keep the pies in the oven during this process. When the oven reaches 325°F, close the door and bake the pies for 5 minutes longer. The pies should still be jiggly in the bull's-eye center but not around the outer edges. If the filling is still too jiggly, leave the pies in the oven for an additional 5 minutes or so.

7. Gently take the pan of crack pies out of the oven and transfer to a rack to cool to room temperature. (You can speed up the cooling process by carefully transferring the pies to the fridge or freezer if you're in a hurry.) Then freeze your pies for at least 3 hours, or overnight, to condense the filling for a dense final product—freezing is the signature technique and result of a perfectly executed crack pie.

8. If not serving the pies right away, wrap well in plastic wrap. In the fridge, they will keep fresh for 5 days; in the freezer, they will keep for 1 month. Transfer the pie(s) from the freezer to the refrigerator to defrost a minimum of 1 hour before you're ready to get in there.

9. Serve your crack pie cold! Decorate your pie(s) with confectioners' sugar, either passing it through a fine sieve or dispatching pinches with your fingers.

oat cookie

MAKES ABOUT 1 QUARTER SHEET PAN

115 g	butter, at room temperature	8 tablespoons (1 stick)
75 g	light brown sugar	⅓ cup tightly packed
40 g	granulated sugar	3 tablespoons
1	egg yolk	
80 g	flour	½ cup
120 g	old-fashioned rolled oats	1½ cups
0.5 g	baking powder	⅛ teaspoon
0.25 g	baking soda	pinch
2 g	kosher salt	½ teaspoon
	Pam or other nonstick cooking spray (optional)	

1. Heat the oven to 350°F.

2. Combine the butter and sugars in the bowl of a stand mixer fitted with the paddle attachment and cream together on medium-high for 2 to 3 minutes, until fluffy and pale yellow in color. Scrape down the sides of the bowl with a

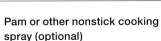
recipe continues

spatula. On low speed, add the egg yolk and increase the speed to medium-high and beat for 1 to 2 minutes, until the sugar granules fully dissolve and the mixture is a pale white.

3. On low speed, add the flour, oats, baking powder, baking soda, and salt. Mix for a minute, until your dough comes together and any remnants of dry ingredients have been incorporated. The dough will be a slightly fluffy, fatty mixture in comparison to your average cookie dough. Scrape down the sides of the bowl.

4. Pam-spray a quarter sheet pan and line with parchment, or just line the pan with a Silpat. Plop the cookie dough in the center of the pan and, with a spatula, spread it out until it is ¼ inch thick. The dough won't end up covering the entire pan; this is OK.

5. Bake for 15 minutes, or until it resembles an oatmeal cookie—caramelized on top and puffed slightly but set firmly. Cool completely before using. Wrapped well in plastic, the oat cookie will keep fresh in the fridge for up to 1 week.

crack pie™ filling

MAKES ENOUGH FOR 2 (10-INCH) CRACK PIES

You *must* use a stand mixer with a paddle attachment to make this filling. It only takes a minute, but it makes all the difference in the homogenization and smooth, silky final product. I repeat: a hand whisk and a bowl or a granny hand mixer will not produce the same results. Also, keep the mixer on low speed through the entire mixing process. If you try to mix the filling on higher speed, you will incorporate too much air and your pie will not be dense and gooey—the essence of crack pie.

300 g	granulated sugar	1½ cups
180 g	light brown sugar	¾ cup tightly packed
20 g	milk powder	¼ cup
24 g	corn powder	¼ cup
6 g	kosher salt	1½ teaspoons
225 g	butter, melted	16 tablespoons (2 sticks)
160 g	heavy cream	¾ cup
2 g	vanilla extract	½ teaspoon
8	egg yolks	

It will be the death of your wildly dense pie filling if there is any bit of egg white in the mixture. I believe the easiest, and best, way to separate an egg is to do so in your hands. You may also use the two half-shells to separate the eggs, but the cracked shells can tear the yolk open, and you may not totally separate all the white. If you do this by hand, you can feel when you get every last bit of white away from the yolk. Remember to wash your hands under warm soapy water for 30 seconds or more before and after you handle raw eggs! Save your egg whites for Peanut Butter Nougat (page 178) or Pistachio Cake (page 84), or cook them up for your doggies, for a shinier coat.

1. Combine the sugar, brown sugar, milk powder, corn powder, and salt in the bowl of a stand mixer fitted with the paddle attachment and mix on low speed until evenly blended.

2. Add the melted butter and paddle for 2 to 3 minutes until all the dry ingredients are moist.

3. Add the heavy cream and vanilla and continue mixing on low for 2 to 3 minutes until any white streaks from the cream have completely disappeared into the mixture. Scrape down the sides of the bowl with a spatula.

4. Add the egg yolks, paddling them into the mixture just to combine; be careful not to aerate the mixture, but be certain the mixture is glossy and homogenous. Mix on low speed until it is.

5. Use the filling right away, or store it in an airtight container in the fridge for up to 1 week.

pecan (or any kind of nut) crack pie™

One of the earliest descriptions we got from our crack pie addicts was, "It's like a pecan pie, without the pecans"—which I secretly hated. It's so much more, and so much less. But one day we finally read between the lines and sarcastically, we thought, made a crack pie with pecans in the pie. It blew my mind a little. There aren't too many boundaries in terms of the variations. So get crazy.

Follow the recipe for crack pie, filling the oat crust with as many or as few pecans (or other nuts) as you have in-house or like (I love it chock-full) before adding the filling. You will need less filling, since nuts will be taking up some of the room in the pie shell.

mixed berry crack pie™

Follow the recipe for crack pie, filling the oat crust with any variety or mixture of berries you have in-house or like before adding the filling. You will need less filling, since berries will be taking up some of the room in the pie shell.

gutter sundae

Conquer this cookbook already?

Too many scraps, leftover crunches, or crumbs?

1. Go to the hardware store. Buy a gutter.

2. Invite your favorite friends and family over.

3. Make a gutter sundae to celebrate.

acknowledgments

Thanks to the ridiculous team behind this cookbook:

• Meehan, my buddy, my brother, my family. I never would have thought such a sophisticated *New York Times* writer would become such a best friend.

• McBrooooom, for being the momentum and hysterics behind the recipes and text. I could not have gotten it done, or had such a great time doing it, without you.

• Gabri, Mark. Mark, Gabri. Life just doesn't feel the same without a "that's what she said." Every 3 minutes. You are the coolest guys around. This book would have been nothing without your vision through the lens and on old-lady decorative plates!

• Kim Witherspoon (cue Whitney Houston's "I Will Always Love You"), thank you for keeping me safe and sound and sane.

• Rica Allannic, for her insights on the manuscript; Judith Sutton, for her conscientious copyediting; Marysarah Quinn, for a design that brought the text to life; and the entire team at Clarkson Potter—including Christine Tanigawa, Joan Denman, Ashley Phillips, Kate Tyler, Sarah Breivogel, Donna Passannante, Allison Malec, Doris Cooper, Lauren Shakely, and Maya Mavjee—for being such wonderful cheerleaders and bringing such drive and dedication to this book.

Dave. Thank you for being crazy enough to see something in me that I couldn't see in myself, and for giving me the space to spread my wings, while kicking me off cliffs hoping like hell I'd learn to fly. I won't ever tell a soul about your soft underbelly. I see you watch over us every day at Milk Bar and smile. Thank you for teaching me to be everything else I never knew how to be before I met you. A leader. A business owner. A boss. An inspiration. A guide.

To the past and present at Noodle, Ssäm, Ko, Má Pêche, the Lab, and Papercut, with a special thanks to the old guard: Qunio, Serp, Hoski, Maslow, Scottie, Kev, Gelman, Kleinman, Cory, Drew, Alex, EJ, and Sue.

wd~50 lead by papa Wylie Dufresne. To everything it's ever been and will become to anyone and everyone. Thank you for existing and for letting me into your inner circle.

To the men strong enough to stand as pastry chefs and crazy enough to have me in their kitchens: Alex Grunert, Sam Mason, Alex Stupak. I can never fully express my gratitude and pride to have worked for you.

Band of Outsiders, for the handsome suit they sent for Louis's Cary Grant moment with Cereal Milk and the inspiring clothing Scott and his team design each season.

Benjamin Wallach, world's best Dairyland Rep.

To my blood, Mom, Dad, and Ang. And the amazing family that followed: Joe, Jason, Mandy, Fede, Nola, Deb, Zhibek, and Dima. Aunts and uncles, grandmothers and grandfathers.

To my makeshift families past and present for giving me homes away from home. To the Bignellis. The Richmond Guard. The old Calhoun's Guard. The Star Island Guard.

To all of our customers at Momofuku and at Milk Bar. Thank you for your support. Thanks for staying on the roller coaster, for riding out the bumps in the road, and for remembering that we're just a team of people who love to bake and feed and please. We do our best for you every day, even on the days when it may not seem good enough.

And to every employee at Milk Bar, future, present, past. Milkmaids and Milkmen. You know who you are. Thanks for believing in it all and in me—for giving blood, sweat, and tears, if only for a shift, or maybe for the long haul. I am eternally grateful.

index